A MANUAL

OF

HINDU PANTHEISM.

THE VEDANTASARA,

TRANSLATED WITH COPIOUS ANNOTATIONS

BY

MAJOR G. A. JACOB

GYAN

Published by

Gyan Publishing House
5, Ansari Road
Daryaganj, New Delhi-110002
Phone: 011-47034999, 9811692060
E-mail: books@gyanbooks.com

Distribution Network
gyanbooks.com
India, USA, Canada, UK, Australia, France

ISBN: 978-81-212-7166-0 (PB)
First Published, 1888

2nd Impression 2024

Printed at: Gyan Press, Delhi.

A MANUAL OF HINDU PANTHEISM
Author: G. A. JACOB

A MANUAL

OF

HINDU PANTHEISM

A MANUAL

OF

HINDU PANTHEISM.

THE VEDÂNTASÂRA,

TRANSLATED WITH COPIOUS ANNOTATIONS

BY

MAJOR G. A. JACOB,
BOMBAY STAFF CORPS;
INSPECTOR OF ARMY SCHOOLS.

Second Edition.

LONDON:
TRÜBNER & CO., LUDGATE HILL.
1888.

Ballantyne Press
BALLANTYNE, HANSON AND CO.
EDINBURGH AND LONDON

PREFACE.

THE design of this little work is to provide for missionaries, and for others who, like them, have little leisure for original research, an accurate summary of the doctrines of the Vedânta. If the people of India can be said to have now any system of religion at all, apart from mere caste observances, it is to be found in the Vedânta philosophy, the leading tenets of which are known to some extent in every village. The subject is therefore one of great importance, and the Vedântasâra is generally acknowledged to be the most satisfactory summary of the modern phases of it.

In the notes, I have endeavoured to furnish a full explanation of every difficulty, and of each point needing elucidation, and in so doing have drawn largely from the writings of well-known Oriental scholars. The text of the Vedântasâra which I have used is that published in Calcutta in 1875 by Pandit Jîvânanda Vidyâsâgara, with the Commentary of Nṛisimhasarasvati.

The following is a list of the works and editions referred to in the translation and notes. I am deeply indebted to Dr. Banerjea's *Dialogues on the Hindu Philosophy*, and to

Dr. Fitzedward Hall's *Rational Refutation of the Hindu Philosophical Systems.* These two are, in my judgment, the most valuable works of their kind in the English language.

Dialogues on the Hindu Philosophy. By Rev. K. M. Banerjea. Williams & Norgate, 1861.

A Rational Refutation of the Hindu Philosophical Systems. By Nehemiah Nilakanṭha Śâstri Gore. Translated by Fitzedward Hall, D.C.L. Calcutta, 1862.

Miscellaneous Essays. By H. T. Colebrooke. New edition, with Notes by Professor Cowell. Trübner & Co., 1873.

The Philosophy of the Upanishads. By Professor A. E. Gough. *Calcutta Review* for 1878.

Original Sanskrit Texts. By J. Muir, D.C.L., LL.D., vols. iii.–v.

Sacred Books of the East. Edited by F. Max Müller, vol. i., *Upanishads.* Clarendon Press, 1879.

Professor H. H. Wilson's *Works*, viz. :—

(a) *Essays on the Religion of the Hindus*, 2 vols. Edited by Dr. R. Rost. Trübner & Co., 1862.

(b) *Essays on Sanskrit Literature*, 3 vols. Edited by Dr. Rost. Trübner & Co., 1864–65.

(c) *Vishnu Purâṇa*, 6 vols. Edited by Dr. Fitzedward Hall. Trübner & Co., 1864–77.

The History of Indian Literature. By Professor Weber, translated from the second German edition. Trübner & Co., 1878.

The Indian Antiquary, vols. i., ii., and iv. Bombay, 1872, 1873, 1875.

Anti-Theistic Theories, the Baird Lecture for 1877. By R. Flint, D.D. Blackwood & Sons, 1879.

Works by Rev. R. Spence Hardy. Published by Williams & Norgate.

(a) *Eastern Monachism.* 1860.

(b) *Legends and Theories of the Buddhists.* 1866.

(c) *Manual of Buddhism*, 2d edition. 1880.

Elphinstone's *History of India*, 6th edition. By E. B. Cowell. J. Murray, 1874.

Works by Dr. Ballantyne.

(a) *The Sânkhya Aphorisms of Kapila*, translated. Bibliotheca Indica Series. Calcutta, 1865.

(b) *The Aphorisms of the Yoga Philosophy*, Book I., translated. Allahabad, 1852.

(c) *The Aphorisms of the Nyâya Philosophy*, translated. Allahabad, 1850.

(d) *A Lecture on the Vedânta.* Allahabad, 1850.

The Aphorisms of Śâṇḍilya. Translated by Professor Cowell. Bibliotheca Indica Series. Calcutta, 1878.

The History of Philosophy. By G. H. Lewes, 2 vols., 4th edition. Longmans & Co., 1871.

Panchadaśî. By Bhâratitîrthavidyâraṇya. Bombay, 1879.

Upadeśasahasrî. By Śankarâchârya. Published in "*The Pandit.*" Benares, 1868-69.

Adhyâtma-Râmâyaṇa. Calcutta, 1872.

Aitareya Brâhmaṇa. Edited and translated by Dr. Haug, 2 vols.

Sânkhyapravachanabhâshya. Edited by Pandit Jibânanda Vidyâsâgara Calcutta.

Kâvya Prakâśa. Edited by Pandit Maheśa Chandra Nyâyaratna. Calcutta, 1866.

Hastâmalaka. Bound up with Jibânanda's edition of Vedântasâra.

Vâkyasudhâ. By Śankarâchârya. Edited by Windischmann in 1833 under the erroneous title of *Bâlabodhinî.* (*Vide* Hall's "*Contribution towards an Index to the Bibliography of Indian Philosophical Systems.*")

Naishkarmyasiddhi. By Sureśwarâchârya. MSS. No. 1103 and 777 in India Office Library.

Pâtanjaladarśana. Edited by Jibânanda Vidyâsâgara. Calcutta, 1874.

Sânkhyasâra. Edited by Fitzedward Hall. Calcutta, 1862. (Bibliotheca Indica Series.)

UPANISHADS.

Kaushîtakî and *Maitrî.* Edited and translated by Professor Cowell. 1861 and 1870.

Kena, Kaṭha Muṇḍaka, Mâṇḍukya, Chhândogya, Taittirîya, Aitareya, Śvetâśvatara, and *Bṛihadâraṇyaka.* Edited by Jibânanda Vidyâsâgara at Calcutta. They are facsimiles of those brought out in the Bibliotheca Indica Series.

Muktika. Edited by Jibânanda Vidyâsâgara.

G. A. J.

TEIGNMOUTH, *August* 1881.

CONTENTS.

VEDÂNTASÂRA.

INTRODUCTORY STANZA.

To the Self, existent, intelligence, bliss, impartite, beyond the range of speech and thought, the substrate of all, I resort for the attainment of the desired thing.[1]

[1] Emancipation.

NOTES ON INTRODUCTORY STANZA.

"All philosophy strives after unity. It is its aim, its task, to reduce complexity to simplicity, the many to the one."[1] The Upanishads tell us that this was the aim of Indian philosophers, and they not always Brahmans, in very early times. In the *Muṇḍaka*, for example, it is related that the illustrious son of Sunaka approached the sage Angiras with due ceremony, and inquired of him what that was which, being known, all things would be known. He was told in reply that the wise regard "the invisible, intangible, unrelated, colourless one, who has neither eyes nor ears, neither hands nor feet, eternal, all-pervading, subtile and undecaying, as the source of all things." This is, of course, Brahma,[2] the so-called Absolute of the Vedânta, the Self of the verse before us; and the system then evolved from the inner consciousness of those early thinkers, but modified it would seem by Śankarâchârya, and so stereotyped by his successors, continues to the present day; and not only so, but whilst the other five schools have well-nigh ceased to exert any appreciable influence, this "has overspread the whole land, overgrown the whole Hindu mind and life."[3]

[1] *Anti-Theistic Theories*, p. 410.

[2] This word is neuter, and must not be confounded with the masculine Brahmâ, a member of the Hindu triad. It is derived from the root *Bṛih*, 'to grow or increase,' and "perhaps its earliest signification was *the expansive force of nature*, regarded as a spiritual power, the power manifested most fully in vegetable, animal, and human life, but everywhere present, though unseen."—*Calcutta Review*, vol. lxvi. p. 14.

[3] *Anti-Theistic Theories*, p. 341.

In this opening verse Brahma is described as

1. *Existent* (*sat*).

The Vedânta postulates three kinds of existence, which it terms true (*pâramârthika*), practical (*vyâvahârika*), and apparent (*prâtibhâsika*). Brahma is the sole representative of the first. The second includes Îśwara, individual souls, heaven, hell, and all phenomena. These are said to be imagined by ignorance, and to have no more true existence than things seen in a dream; but men have practical dealings with them as if they truly existed, so they are admitted to exist practically or conventionally. The third class comprises such things as a mirage, nacre mistaken for silver, or a snake imagined in a rope, which are the result of some defect, such as short-sight, &c., in addition to ignorance. Yet it is believed that "when a man on seeing nacre, takes it for silver, apparent silver is *really produced!*" All these then are, from certain standpoints, real existences; but, to him who has true knowledge, the first alone is real.[1] This theory of existences is intended to explain away the finite and establish the infinite; but it cannot be admitted to have been successful. The existence of an invisible Being, who is entirely out of relation to the world, and devoid of apprehension, will, activity, and all other qualities, cannot possibly be established.

2. *Intelligence* (*chit* or *chaitanya*).

This is the most common synonym of Brahma, but he is also spoken of—as, for example, in the *Taittirîya Upanishad* (p. 56)—as 'cognition' or 'knowledge' (*jnâna*). It must, however, be clearly understood that *he is not a cognizer or intelligent*. In commenting on the passage of the Upanishad just referred to, Śankarâchârya says:—

[1] *Rational Refutation*, sec. iii. chap. i.

"Knowledge is here an abstract, indicating cognition, not the cognitive subject, being predicated of the ultimate along with truth and infinity. Truth and infinity would be incompatible with it did it imply a subject of cognition. If the pure idea were susceptible of modifications, how could it be pure and infinite? That is infinite which cannot be demarcated in any direction. If it were a knowing subject, it would be limited by its objects and its cognitions. . . . The knowledge of the absolute spirit, like the light of the sun, or like the heat in fire, is nought else than the absolute essence itself."[1]

In the *Mâṇḍukya Upanishad* (ver. 7), too, Brahma is said to be "neither[2] internally nor externally cognitive, neither conscious nor unconscious." This tenet is a necessity. For if Brahma were conscious, there would be objects of consciousness, which would involve dualism; for "wherever there is consciousness there is relation, and wherever there is relation there is dualism."[3] The Hindu pantheist, therefore, allying himself with "a scepticism which denies the validity of the primary perceptions and fundamental laws of mind,"[4] calmly annihilates the phenomenal, and with it his own self-consciousness, by calling it all illusory. It must be understood that the only ground for supposing Brahma to be 'intelligence,' is, that, in the state of practical existence, cognition of an object can only be effected by means of the internal organ, and that organ is declared to be itself unintelligent and to need an illuminator. The self-luminous Brahma is that illuminator! "It is not meant, however, that Brahma, by a voluntary exercise of

[1] *Calcutta Review*, vol. lxvi. p. 19.
[2] *Ibid.*, p. 29.
[3] *Anti-Theistic Theories*, p. 423.
[4] *Ibid.*, p. 419.

his power, illumines that organ, for Brahma has no such power. The idea intended is, that the internal organ, simply by reason of its proximity to Brahma, who is unconscious, becomes illuminated, just as iron moves when brought near the magnet."[1] 'Intelligence,' therefore, means simply 'self-luminousness,' and its existence is surmised merely on the ground named above! But the internal organ[2] is a portion of the phenomenal, and therefore illusory. So too must be its illuminator. Brahma, therefore, as 'intelligence,' is not established.

3. *Bliss* (*ânanda*).

This has been characterised as "a bliss without the fruition of happiness," and rightly so. For absorption into Brahma is described as a permanent state "resembling precisely that of deep sleep,"—"a condition of insensibility,"—in which the emancipated spirit is without a body, mind, or cognition! Where is there any room in such a state for joy? "But what, in that case," says the author of the *Sânkhya-pravachana-bhâshya*, "becomes of the scripture which lays down that soul is happiness? The answer is: 'Because of there being *cessation of misery*, only in a loose acceptation does the term happiness denote soul.' . . . To move ambition in the dull or ignorant, the emancipated state, which really is *stoppage of misery*, Soul itself, is lauded to them by the Veda as happiness."[3] Brahma, then, as joy, is wholly a product of the imagination.

4. *Impartite* (*akhaṇḍa*).

According to the commentator *Nṛisimhasarasvati*, this

[1] *Rational Refutation*, pp. 214–216.

[2] In Sanskrit, *antahkaraṇa*. It consists of *manas*, *buddhi*, *ahankâra*, and *chitta*, and yet is unintelligent!

[3] *Rational Refutation*, pp. 33, 34.

term means "devoid of anything of a like kind or of a different kind, and without internal variety." A tree, for example, has the 'internal variety' of leaves, flowers, and fruit; it has things 'of a like kind,' in other trees—and things 'of a different kind,' in stones,[1] &c. But Brahma is not so, he being absolute and unchangeable unity. It is from the standpoint of true existence that he is regarded as impartite and solitary; for, from that of practical existence, he is appropriated to countless internal organs and underlies all phenomena.

5. *Substrate of all* (*akhilâdhâra*).

He is the substrate only in the way that nacre is of apparent silver, or that a rope is of the snake imagined in it; and, like the silver and the snake, the world is but a *vivartta* or illusory effect. Its illusory-material cause is Brahma, and ignorance its material cause. The writers of the Upanishads, *i.e.*, the Vedantists of the old school, were undoubtedly *pariṇâmavâdins*, or believers in the *reality* of the world of perception; and, with them, Brahma was not its substrate or illusory-material cause, but the material from which it was evolved or developed, as the web from a spider, as foam from water, or as curd from milk.[2] The passage quoted above from the Muṇḍaka Upanishad seems clearly to teach this doctrine when setting forth Brahma as the absolute unity, which being known, all things are known; and the context adds that "as a spider throws out and retracts [its web], as herbs spring up in the ground, and as hair is produced on the living person, so is the universe derived from the undecaying one" (i. 1, 7). It seems to be distinctly taught, too, in the *Chhândogya Upanishad*. The sixth

[1] *Panchadaśî*, ii. 20. [2] *Miscellaneous Essays*, i. 375, 376.

book opens with a dialogue between a Brahman named Áruṇi and his son Śvetaketu, who, at twenty-four years of age, has returned home on the completion of a twelve years' course of Vedic study. Seeing him full of conceit, his father asks him whether he had sought from his teacher that instruction by which the unheard becomes heard, the unthought thought, the unknown known. On the son's confessing that he had not sought it, the father says, "My dear, as by one clod of clay all that is made of clay is known, the difference being only a name, arising from speech, but the truth being that all is clay; and as, my dear, by one nugget of gold all that is made of gold is known, the difference being only a name, arising from speech, but the truth being that all is gold; and as, my dear, by one pair of nail-scissors all that is made of iron is known, the difference being only a name, arising from speech, but the truth being that all is iron—thus, my dear, is that instruction."[1] That is to say, Brahma being known as material cause, all things are known. The son then remarks that his teacher could not have known this doctrine, and asks his father to explain it further. The latter then goes on to say, "In the beginning, my dear, this was the existent, one only, without a second. Some say that in the beginning, this was the non-existent, one only, without a second; and from the non-existent the existent arose. But how could it be thus, my dear; how could the existent arise from the non-existent? In the beginning, my dear, this was indeed the existent, one only, without a second." Śankarâchârya says that 'this'[2] refers to 'the

[1] *Sacred Books of the East*, i. 92.

[2] Prof. Max Müller, in his translation, omits 'this' altogether, and so completely changes the sense of the passage.

universe' (*jagat*), and that 'in the beginning' means 'before production' (*prâgutpatteh*). The drift of the passage then surely is that this world, *a reality*, before its evolution, existed potentially in Brahma, its material cause. It, in fact, "proves the reality of the cause from the reality of the effect, and so declares the reality, not the falseness of all."[1] In the same Upanishad (iii. 14, 1), we find the words, "All this is indeed Brahma, being produced from, resolved into, and existing in him;" and the opening words of the *Aitareya Upanishad* are, "In the beginning this was the self, one only;" and in both cases, as before, 'this' is said to refer to the world of perception, which is treated as a reality.

In his valuable essay on the Vedânta, Colebrooke shows, by ample quotations, that this view of the world's reality and of Brahma's material causativity was propounded by the early Vedantic teachers, including Śankarâchârya himself; and he considered the doctrine of Mâyâ, or the world's unreality, to be "a graft of a later growth," uncountenanced by the aphorisms of the Vedânta or by the gloss of Śankarâchârya. The learned editor of the new edition of Colebrooke's essays thinks this "hardly correct" as regards Śankara, but adds, "There can hardly be a question as to the fact that the original *Vedânta* of the earlier *Upanishads* and of the *Sûtras* did not recognize the doctrine of *Mâyâ*. The earliest school seems to have held Brahma to be the material cause of the world in a grosser sense." As regards Śankarâchârya, the fact is that different portions of his comments on the aphorisms are mutually conflicting. For example, in one place he ridicules the idea of an infinite series of works and worlds

[1] *Aphorisms of Sâṇḍilya*, translated by Cowell, p. 42.

subsisting in the relation of cause and effect, and then, elsewhere, distinctly advocates it. Again, when opposing the idealism of the Buddhists, he strongly maintains the *reality* of objects of perception, rebutting the objections advanced against it, and supports the tenet of the material causativity of Brahma; whilst on another occasion he accepts the theory of *Mâyâ*.[1]

6. '*Beyond the range of speech or thought.*'

The following are some of the Vedic texts on this point:—"From whom words turn back, together with the mind, not reaching him" (*Taittirîya*, ii. 9). "The eye goes not thither, nor speech, nor mind" (*Kena*, i. 3). "Unthinkable, unspeakable" (*Mâṇḍukya*, 7).

The Vedantist creed, as held since the time of Śankarâchârya, *i.e.*, during the last thousand years, may, then, be thus summed up:—"Brahma alone—a spirit; essentially existent, intelligence and joy; void of all qualities and of all acts; in whom there is no consciousness such as is denoted by 'I,' 'thou,' and 'it;' who apprehends no person or thing, nor is apprehended of any; who is neither parviscient nor omniscient; neither parvipotent nor omnipotent; who has neither beginning nor end; immutable and indefectible—is the true entity. All besides himself, the entire universe, is false, that is to say, is nothing whatsoever. Neither has it ever existed, nor does it now exist, nor will it exist at any time future."[2]

It is very interesting to note the likeness between Brahma thus portrayed and the 'Being' of Parmenides, who was the contemporary of Buddha and Confucius. "Being, he argued, is absolutely one. It is not an

[1] *Dialogues on Hindu Philosophy*, pp. 109, 123, and chaps. vii. and viii.
[2] *Rational Refutation*, p. 176.

abstract unity, but the only reality. It is so that it alone is. Being, he further affirmed, is continuous and indivisible; it is everywhere like to itself, and everywhere alike present. Were there parts in being there would be plurality, and being would not be one—that is, would not be being. There can be no differences or distinctions in being; for what is different and distinct from being must be not-being, and not-being is not. . . . Being, he likewise held, is identical with thought. It could not otherwise be absolutely one. Thought, he said, is the same thing as being. Thought must be being; for being exists, and non-being is nothing." "His not-being did not mean non-existence, but all that sense and ordinary thought apprehend as existence; it included earth, air, ocean, and the minds of men."[1] This 'being' is exactly the *sat*, *chit*, and *akhaṇḍa* of the Vedânta, whilst the idea of 'not-being' coincides entirely with its *vyâvahârikî* or *prâtibhâsikî sattâ*.

[1] *Anti-Theistic Theories*, p. 353. Cf. also Lewes' *Hist. of Philosophy*, i. 56.

I.

Having saluted my preceptor, who, from his having got rid of the notion of duality, is significantly named Adwayânanda, I will now propound the essence of the Vedânta, according to my conception of it.

The Vedânta doctrine is based upon the Upanishads, and is likewise supported by the *Śârîraka sûtras* and other works.[1]

[1] Such as the Bhagavad-Gîtâ, &c.

NOTES ON SECTION I.

1. *Vedânta.*

This "literally signifies 'conclusion of the Veda,' and bears reference to the Upanishads, which are, for the most part, terminating sections of the Vedas to which they belong. It implies, however, *the doctrine* derived from them, and extends to books of sacred authority, in which that doctrine is thence deduced; and, in this large acceptation, it is the end and scope of the Vedas." [1]

2. *Śârîraka sûtras.*

This is a collection of aphorisms composed by Bâdarâyaṇa, and forms one of the six Darśanas or Systems of Philosophy. The word *śârîraka* is said to be derived from the noun *śarîraka*, which the commentator calls a contemptuous (*kutsita*) form of *śarîra*, 'body,' and means 'embodied' (soul). Śankarâchârya's interpretation of these aphorisms and of the Upanishads, is the real authority for the tenets of the modern school.

Prior to the rise of Buddhism, dogma and ritual held undisputed sway. The followers of that heresy, however, presumed to appeal to reason, and their system was at once stigmatised as 'the science of reason' (*hetuśâstra*), which was then synonymous with heresy. This was doubtless the first systematic departure from the Mantras and Brâhmaṇas; but the Brahmans were soon compelled to follow suit, and to them we owe the six so-called orthodox schools of Indian philosophy. I say 'so-called,' for the teaching of the Systems is no less a departure from

[1] Colebrooke's *Essays*, i. 351.

the old religion than Buddhism is; but they profess respect for the Vedas, whilst the Buddhists openly repudiate them. The following remarks by a native scholar will be of interest here:—

"In justice to the founders of our schools, we must confess that the opinions which they embodied in their systems had probably long been floating in the popular mind. The Buddhist defection had no doubt produced a spirit of scepticism from which the authors of the Sûtras were not wholly free. And they, perhaps, laboured to give such a shape to those sceptical opinions as might be consistent with the supremacy of the Brahmanical order. Two things, they thought, were necessary for the maintenance of that supremacy—the toleration of the Vedas and the substitution of metaphysical speculations for the too frequent performance of the Vedic ritual. Without the first, the foundation of Brahmanical supremacy would be cut away. Without the second, the Brahmanical mind would be doomed to a state of perpetual imbecility, familiar only with ceremonial observances, and utterly unable to meet the challenges put forth by sceptical heretics in the arena of controversy. Not that there was much essential difference in point of doctrine between the heretical and some of the orthodox schools. If Kapila could assert the non-existence of a Supreme Being, and if Kaṇâda could attribute the primal action of eternal atoms to *adṛishṭa,* I cannot see how there could be a marked difference of opinion between them and the heretics."[1]

The Bhagavad-Gîtâ is accounted most orthodox, but this

[1] *Dialogues on Hindu Philosophy,* p. 73. For further discussion of this interesting question see Wilson's *Essays on the Religion of the Hindus,* ii. 85–87.

is what it says of the Vedas (ii. 42–46):—"A flowery doctrine, promising the reward of works performed in this embodied state, presenting numerous ceremonies, with a view to future gratification and glory, is prescribed by unlearned men, devoted to the injunctions of the Veda, assertors of its exclusive importance, lovers of enjoyment, and seekers after paradise. The restless minds of the men who, through this flowery doctrine, have become bereft of wisdom and are ardent in the pursuit of future gratification and glory, are not applied to contemplation. The Vedas have for their objects the three qualities; but be thou, Arjuna, free from these three qualities. . . . As great as is the use of a well which is surrounded on all sides by overflowing waters, so great [and no greater] is the use of the Vedas to a Brâhman endowed with true knowledge."[1] King Aśoka gave the death-blow to animal sacrifices in the third century before Christ, as various rock and pillar inscriptions bear witness; but the demolition of the rest of the fabric was effected by the orthodox philosophers, who spoke of it as "inferior science!"

3. *The Upanishads.*

These are short speculative treatises appended to the Vedas, and are about 235 in number.[2] Only thirteen of them, however, are really important or much quoted. They are the following:—*Ṛigveda:* Aitareya and Kauśîtaki. *Sâmaveda:* Kena and Chhândogya. *White Yajurveda:* Îśâ and Bṛihadâranyaka. *Black Yajurveda:* Kaṭha, Maitrî, Taittirîya, and Śvetâśvatara. *Atharvaveda:* Praśna, Muṇḍaka, and Mâṇḍukya.

The word *Upanishad* is derived by native authors from

[1] Muir's *Sanskrit Texts*, iii. 32.

[2] *Hist. of Indian Literature*, p. 155 (*note*).

the root *shad*, 'to destroy' (preceded by the prepositions *upa*, 'near,' and *ni*, 'down'), and is held to be that body of teaching which destroys illusion and reveals the Absolute. Professor Max Müller, however, considers this explanation to be "wilfully perverse," and derives it from *sad*, 'to sit down,' "so that it would express the idea of session, or assembly of pupils sitting down near their teacher to listen to his instruction."[1] These tracts are thus described by Professor Cowell:—"The Upanishads are usually in the form of dialogue; they are generally written in prose with occasional snatches of verse, but sometimes they are in verse altogether. They have no system or method; the authors are poets, who throw out their unconnected and often contradictory rhapsodies on the impulse of the moment, and have no thought of harmonizing to-day's feelings with those of yesterday or to-morrow. . . . Through them all runs an unmistakable spirit of Pantheism, often in its most offensive form, as avowedly overriding all moral considerations; and it is this which has produced the general impression that the religion of the Veda is monotheistic."[2]

[1] *Sacred Books of the East*, vol. i. p. lxxx.

[2] Elphinstone's *Hist. of India*, p. 282.

II.

As this tract has for its subject the Vedânta, and has clearly the same *praecognita*[1] as that system, it is unnecessary to consider them in detail. [But lest any one should not have read the large treatise, I may say that] the præcognita in that system are—

I. The qualified person (*adhikârin*).
II. The subject (*vishaya*).
III. The relation (*sambandha*).
IV. The purpose (*prayojana*).

I. '*The qualified person*' is one who possesses due intelligence; that is, one who, by reading the Vedas and Vedângas according to rule, either in this life or in a former one, has obtained a general idea of the meaning of the whole,—who, by performing the constant and occasional rites, the penances, and devotional exercises, and abstaining from things done with desire of reward and from those forbidden

[1] Ballantyne renders this by "moving considerations." The original is *anubandha*.

has got rid of all sin and so thoroughly cleansed his mind,—and who is possessed of the four means.

'The things done with desire of reward' (or 'optional things,' *kâmya*) are the Jyotishṭoma sacrifice and other things of a similar kind, which are the means of procuring heaven and other desirable things.

The 'forbidden things' (*nishiddha*) are the slaying of a Brâhman and the like, which result in hell and other undesirable things.

The 'constant rites' (*nitya*) are the Sandhyâ prayers and the like, which cause ruin if left undone.

The 'occasional rites' (*naimittika*) are such as the birth-sacrifice following the birth of a son, and such like.

The 'penances' (*prâyaśchitta*) are such as the *Chândrâyaṇa* and others, which are used only for the removal of sin.

The 'devotional exercises' (*upâsana*) are such as the system of Śâṇdilya and the like, consisting of mental efforts directed towards Brahma with qualities.

The principal object of the constant and occasional rites and of the penances is the purification of the intellect; that of the devotional exercises is the concentration of the mind. As it is written in the Veda, "Him, the Self, Brâhmans seek to know by means of the reading of the Veda and by sacrifice" (*Bṛihadâranyaka Upanishad*, 4. 4. 22); and in the Smṛiti, "By religious acts he destroys sin" (*Manu*, xii. 104).

An incidental result of the constant and occasional rites and of the devotional exercises is the acquisition of the abode of the progenitors and of the abode of Brahma; as the Veda says, "By works, the abode of the progenitors; by knowledge, the abode of the gods" (*Bṛihadâranyaka*, 1. 5. 16).

The 'four means' (*sâdhana*) are (*a*.) discrimination between eternal and non-eternal substances, (*b*.) indifference to the enjoyment of rewards here and hereafter, (*c*.) the possession of quiescence, self-restraint, &c., and (*d*.) desire for release.

(*a*.) 'Discrimination between eternal and non-eternal substances' is the discerning that Brahma is the only eternal substance, and that all else besides him is non-eternal.

(*b*.) 'Indifference to the enjoyment of rewards here or hereafter' is complete indifference to the enjoyment of the things of this life, such as garlands, sandals, and other objects of sense,—and of those pertaining to the next world, such as nectar and other sensuous objects,—because, being the result of works, they are non-eternal.

(*c*.) 'Quiescence, self-restraint, &c.,' are quiescence, self-restraint, abstinence, endurance, contemplative concentration, and faith.

'Quiescence' is the restraining of the mind from objects of sense opposed to hearing, &c.

'Self-restraint' is the turning away of the external organs from objects opposed to that hearing.

'Abstinence' is the continued abstaining of the external organs from sensuous objects opposed to that hearing, after they have been turned away from them; or it may be the abandonment of prescribed acts in a legitimate manner [*i.e.*, by becoming an ascetic].

'Endurance' is bearing the polarities of heat and cold, &c.

'Contemplative concentration' is the fixing of the restrained mind on hearing and such like things which are helpful to it.

'Faith' is belief in the utterances of the spiritual teacher and of the Vedânta.

(*d*.) 'Desire for release' is the longing for emancipation.

A man of this kind, the possessor of due intelligence, is '*a qualified person.*' As the Veda says, "The tranquil, restrained man, &c." (*Bṛihadâraṇyaka Upanishad*, 4. 4. 26); and as it is said elsewhere, "To the seeker of emancipation, who is tranquil in mind, who has subdued his senses, whose sins are gone, who is obedient and virtuous, and who, long and continuously, has followed a teacher, is this to be taught" (*Upadeśasahasrî*, ver. 324).

II. '*The subject*' is the unity of souls and of Brahma, as pure intelligence, a fact which is to be demonstrated; for this is the purport of all Vedânta treatises.

III. '*The relation*' between that unity, the thing to be proved, and the proof derived from the Upanishads which set it forth, is that which is characterised as the condition of 'the explainer and thing to be explained.'

IV. '*The purpose*' is the removal of the ignorance regarding the unity which is to be demonstrated, and the acquisition of the joy which is the essence of Brahma. As the Veda says, "The knower of Self passes beyond sorrow" (*Chhândogy Upanishad*, 7. 1. 3); and again, "He who knows Brahma becomes Brahma" (*Muṇḍaka*, 3. 2. 9).

As a man with a hot head goes to the water, so this qualified person, scorched by the fires of mundane existence, with its births, deaths, and other ills, takes a bundle of firewood in his hands and approaches a spiritual teacher versed in the Vedas and intent upon Brahma, and becomes his follower. As it is said in the Veda, "In order to know Him, he should go with fuel in his hands to a teacher learned in the Vedas and intent on Brahma" (*Muṇḍaka Upanishad*, I. 2. 12). That teacher,[1] with great kindness, instructs him by the method of illusory attribution (*adhyâropa*), followed by its withdrawal (*apavâda*). As it is written in the Veda, "To him, on drawing nigh with truly calmed mind and sense subdued, that learned one should[2] so expound, in truth, the Brahma lore, that he may know the true and undecaying Male" (*Muṇḍaka*, I. 2. 13).

1 In commenting on the foregoing passage, Śankarâchârya lays stress on the need of a *teacher*, and says "*S'âstrajno'pi svâtantryeṇa Brahmajnânânveshaṇam na kuryât*," "Even though a man know the scriptures, he should not attempt to acquire the knowledge of Brahma independently." In *Panchadasî*, iv. 39–41, too, it is pointed out that, though at the *pralaya* duality will disappear of itself, yet deliverance from future births is not to be had without a previously acquired knowledge of Brahma, which knowledge it will be impossible to gain then, because there will be neither teacher nor scriptures!

2 *Provâcha* is here equivalent to *prabrûyât*, says Śankara.

NOTES ON SECTION II.

1. The foregoing shows the compromise made by the philosophers with the pre-existing systems of ritual and devotion. They retained them, but merely, they said, as means of purifying the intellect for the reception of the higher truths,[1] a process similar to the polishing of a tarnished mirror so as to fit it to reflect an image.

"Whoever, therefore, hearing that the Vedântins believe in Brahma without qualities, infers that they reject Vishnu, Śiva, and the rest of the pantheon, and that they discountenance idolatry and such things, and that they count the Purâṇas and similar writings false, labours under gross error."[2] In fact, it is laid down in *Panchadaśî*, vi. 206–209, that any kind of god or demigod, or anything in the animal, vegetable, or mineral kingdom, may be properly worshipped as a portion of Îśwara, and that such worship will bring a reward proportioned to the dignity of the object worshipped.

Worship is natural to man; and in making a compromise with the theologians the philosophers merely acknowledged this fact. Their system, however, like that of Buddha, had no object of worship, or indeed anything "to elicit and sustain a religious life;" so they were compelled "to crave the help of polytheism, and to treat the foullest orgies and cruellest rites of idolatry as acts of reasonable worship paid indirectly to the sole and supreme Being."[3]

[1] Cf. *Muṇḍaka Upanishad*, 3. 1. 5. [2] *Rational Refutation*, p. 195.
[3] *Anti-Theistic Theories*, p. 389.

It is laid down, however, in *Panchadaśî*, iv. 43–46, that as soon as the knowledge of the truth is obtained, the sacred writings themselves, as a portion of the unreal dualism, are to be abandoned, just as a torch is extinguished when one has no further need of it, or as the husk is thrown away by one who merely wants the grain! The dishonesty of Pantheism is thus clearly seen. For "if it look upon the popular deities as mere fictions of the popular mind, its association with polytheism can only mean a conscious alliance with falsehood, the deliberate propagation of lies. If, on the other hand, it regard them as really manifestations of the Absolute Being, it must believe this on the authority of revelation or tradition,"[1] the whole of which the Vedantist classes with unrealities!

2. '*In this life or in a former one.*'

It is this tenet of a succession of births that furnishes the *raison d'être* of the systems of philosophy, as their professed aim is to provide a way of deliverance from them. The doctrine of metempsychosis still prevails in India, Ceylon, Burmah, Tibet, Tartary, and China, and is accepted, therefore, by the larger portion of the human race. It would be a source of much satisfaction to us if we could discover the time and place of its birth. It was not held by the Aryan family or by the early Indian settlers, for the Vedas recognise the continued existence of the soul after death in some heavenly sphere, and contain no distinct reference whatever to the fact of transmigration.[2] Its first appearance in orthodox writings is in the Chhândogya and Bṛihadâraṇyaka Upanishads, which

[1] *Anti-Theistic Theories*, p. 390.

[2] Wilson's *Essays on Sanskrit Literature*, iii. 345.

are believed by Professor Weber to have been composed at about the same period, the former in the west of Hindustan, the latter in the east. He, however, refers them to a "comparatively recent date," and tells us that the doctrines promulgated in the latter by Yâjnavalkya are "completely Buddhistic."[1] That being the case, we may justly consider these two treatises to have been post-Buddhistic; and there then remains no ancient orthodox composition which can claim to have set forth the doctrine of transmigration prior to the appearance of Buddha. It is embodied, it is true, in Manu's Code of Laws, for which a very high antiquity has been claimed; but there can be no reasonable doubt that the present redaction of it was posterior to the rise of Buddhism, and some would even bring it down to as late a time as the third century before Christ.[2] But even if it be true that the doctrine was first publicly taught by Buddha, it by no means follows that he was the originator of it, and that it had not been a matter of speculation long before his time. As a matter of fact, the theory of the transmigration of *soul* was assuredly not his, for he totally denied the existence of soul. What he taught was the transmigration of *karma*, that is, of the aggregate of all a man's actions in every state of existence in which he has lived.[3] According to him, a man is made up of five aggregates (Sanskrit, *skandha*; Pâli, *khanda*) of properties or qualities, viz., 1. *Rûpa*, organised body, comprising twenty-eight divisions; 2. *Vedanâ*, sensation, comprising eighteen divisions; 3.

[1] *History of Indian Literature*, pp. 71, 73, 285.

[2] Elphinstone's *History of India*, 6th ed., by Cowell, p. 249. The most probable date of the death of Buddha is 477 B.C.

[3] Hardy's *Legends and Theories of the Buddhists*, p. 164.

Sañjnâ, perception, comprising six divisions; 4. *Sanskâra*, discrimination, comprising fifty-two divisions; and 5. *Vijnâna*, consciousness, comprising eighty-nine divisions. At death, these five are broken up and dispersed, never to be reunited. But, besides *karma*, there is another property inherent in all sentient beings, named *upâdâna*, or 'cleaving to existing objects;' and these two survive the dispersion of the aggregates and produce a new being. "By *upâdâna* a new existence is produced, but the means of its operation is controlled by the *karma* with which it is connected. It would sometimes appear that *upâdâna* is the efficient cause of reproduction, and that at other times it is *karma*. But in all cases it is the *karma* that appoints whether the being to be produced shall be an insect in the sunbeam, a worm in the earth, a fish in the sea, a fowl in the air, a beast in the forest, a man, a restless *dewa* or *brahma* of the celestial world."[1]

Such is the Buddhist notion of transmigration; and it would be more reasonable to suppose it to have been an adaptation of the usual theory than to regard the latter as modified from it.

The other Asiatic countries named above obtained the doctrine, together with the rest of Buddhism, from India, and can therefore give us no help in our search. Turning to Europe, we find the metempsychosis amongst the philosophy of Pythagoras, who is supposed to have been born some time between 604 and 520 B.C.[2] His life is "shrouded in the dim magnificence of legends," amongst which we should doubtless class the theory of his having

[1] Hardy's *Manual of Buddhism*, p. 409.

[2] Buddha is supposed to have lived eighty years, and so was probably born about 557 B.C. *Ibid.*, p. 366.

visited India. Still the similarity of much of his system to that of Indian philosophers is very curious, and Colebrooke thought that it was borrowed from them.

With regard, however, to the supposed Eastern origin of much of that philosopher's teaching, Mr. George Henry Lewes thus wrote: "Every dogma in it has been traced to some prior philosophy. Not a vestige will remain to be called the property of the teacher himself if we restore to the Jews, Indians, Egyptians, Chaldeans, Phœnicians, nay, even Thracians, those various portions which he is declared to have borrowed from them. All this pretended plagiarism we incline to think extremely improbable. Pythagoras was a successor of Anaximander, and his doctrines, in so far as we can gather their leading tendency, were but a continuation of that abstract and deductive philosophy of which Anaximander was the originator."[1]

But this by no means exhausts the field for inquiry, for Egypt is known to have held the theory of transmigration, possibly before it was taught in Greece; but whether it was introduced from without, or evolved from the inner consciousness of the nation itself, we cannot determine. We have to acknowledge ourselves completely baffled, then, in our search for the birthplace of this important dogma; and whether it originated in the West or in the East, or arose simultaneously in both worlds, it is absolutely impossible to say, and we must be content to leave the question in the thick haze which impenetrably enshrouds it.

3. '*Reading the Veda,*' &c.

The study of the Veda and the practice of its ritual

[1] *History of Philosophy*, 4th edition, i. 26.

being prerequisites to the initiation into the higher mysteries, the advantages offered by philosophy were beyond the reach of the masses, and for them something simpler and more attractive was provided. But the real object of the provision thus made, whether for the learned or the ignorant, for the few or the many, was to put forth a counter-attraction to the system of Śâkya Muni.

When we think of the wonderful deliverance that had been offered by Buddhism to the priest-ridden communities of India, of the vast number of its adherents, and of its great power, which so effectually checked Brahman supremacy for centuries, it seems almost incredible that it should ever have succumbed, and have been driven beyond the Himalayas. Yet so it was. Possibly its very success engendered indolence and inactivity on the part of those who ought actively to have maintained and propagated it;[1] or its extreme simplicity and strict morality may at length have proved irksome and rendered it unpopular;[2] or the weakness necessarily inherent in a religion without a God to be loved and worshipped may have been at length manifested in it, and so have opened the way for the astute Brahmans, who were ever on the watch for opportunities for recovering their long-lost sway. But be this as it may, the opportunity came, and the means employed for eradicating the heresy were twofold, namely, persecution and the introduction of a sensuous and attractive worship.

The former is supposed to have been commenced as early as the third century of our era, but to have been actively

[1] Wilson's *Essays on the Religion of the Hindus*, ii. 367.

[2] Weber's *History of Indian Literature*, p. 289 (*note*).

and more successfully carried on during the fifth and sixth centuries. The probability of the persecution of the latter period is remarkably strengthened by the fact that Buddhism received a fresh impulse in China in A.D. 519, was introduced into the Corea in A.D. 530, into Japan in A.D. 540–550, and into Java during the sixth and seventh centuries, which witnessed the arrival of large numbers of Hindu emigrants.[1] We have evidence of the fact of the decline of Buddhism in those early centuries from the diary of the Chinese pilgrim Hiouen Thsang, who came to India in the year 629 A.D. to study original Buddhist works, and during his residence of fourteen or fifteen years travelled over a great part of the country.

He found large numbers of flourishing monasteries, conspicuous amongst which was that of Nâlanda (north-east of Gayâ), which contained 10,000 resident monks, some of whom were "visitors from all parts of India, who had come to study the abstruser Buddhist books under its renowned teachers;" but on the other hand, there were vast numbers deserted and in ruins, whilst Hindu temples abounded and 'heretics' swarmed in every city.[2]

The struggle was renewed, at the end of the seventh century, by the famous Mimânsaka, Kumârila Bhaṭṭa, who was regarded as "an incarnation of Kârtikeya, the object of whose descent was the extirpation of the Saugatas" (Buddhists), and ended in the complete expulsion of the latter from the Deckan. The great controversialist Śankara Âchârya, too, who lived a century later, is supposed by some to have used sterner weapons than the pen in demolishing heretics; but, on the other hand, his

[1] Wilson's *Essays on Sanskrit Literature*, iii. 198.

[2] Elphinstone's *History of India*, 6th ed., by Cowell, pp. 288–299.

"mild character" and "uniformly gentle and tolerant" disposition, as well as the absence from his writings of all mention of the persecution of his opponents, have been brought forward in disproof of the charge.[1] Notwithstanding the efforts of their enemies to uproot them, the Buddhists were still found on the Coromandel Coast in the eighth and ninth centuries, and in Guzerat, and on the throne of Bengal in the twelfth century; but after that they were heard of no more. In the fourteenth century they were not found south of Kashmir, and by the sixteenth century they appear to have been rarely met with even there.[2]

The attempt to suppress Buddhism by fire and sword was supplemented, however, by other measures, in order to place reviving Brahmanical supremacy on a firm basis. These, somewhat after the fashion of Balaam's tactics for the seduction and ruin of Israel, consisted of the introduction of an extremely sensuous and debasing form of Krishna-worship, together with the cults of certain female deities.[3] "The Brahmans saw, on regaining their supremacy after the fall of the rival school, that it would be impossible to enlist the popular sympathy in their favour without some concessions to the Śudras. They accordingly pitched on the well-known, and perhaps already deified, character of Krishna, and set it up as an object of universal worship. And in order to make it the more fascinating to the popular mind, and to give that mind a strong impulse in a direction the very opposite of Buddhism, they invested their new god with those infirmities of the flesh from which Śâkya Muni is said to have been

[1] *Essays on Sanskrit Literature*, iii. 191–197. [2] *Ibid.*, p. 225.
[3] Weber's *History of Indian Literature*, p. 289 (*note*).

somewhat unnaturally free. The rude mind of the populace, devoid of education, is easily led in the direction of sensuality, and whereas Buddha had observed rigid chastity in the midst of several thousand damsels resident in his own palace, Krishna was represented as the very antithesis of Buddha, deliberately going about to seek, seduce, carry off, or procure by other means many thousands of females from different parts of the country. . . . Whatever ideas, expressive of the divine majesty, they could themselves imagine, and whatever sentiments, borrowed from other quarters, struck their fancies as suitable for a popular system, they freely received in the construction of their new idol. And thus the very character which had injured so many husbands and stained the purity of so many households, was otherwise described as the Lord of sacrifices, the greatest destroyer of sin, and the deliverer of the world."[1] The success which attended this scheme was very marked, and continues undiminished to this day.

The time of the introduction of Krishna-worship having, however, formed a subject of debate amongst scholars, it

[1] K. M. Banerjea's *Dialogues on the Hindu Philosophy*, p. 520. In *Bhagavad Gîtâ*, iv. 8, Krishna is made to speak of himself as appearing in every age for the complete deliverance of the saintly, the overthrow of the wicked, and the establishment of righteousness; and in xviii. 66 as the deliverer from all sin! The Bhâgavata Purâṇa is said to have been related by the Sage Śuka to King Parîkshit, who, after listening to the account of Krishna's debaucheries, is said to have inquired how it was that he who became incarnate "for the establishment of virtue" and the repression of vice, and who was "the expounder, author, and guardian of the bulwarks of righteousness," was guilty of such corrupt practices. The reply to this very proper question was as follows:—"The transgression of virtue and the daring acts which are witnessed in superior beings (*Îsvarâṇâm*) must not be charged as faults to these glorious persons. . . . Let no one other than a superior being ever even in thought practise the

may be well to dwell upon it further. It should be stated at the outset that there is an important difference between the mere deification of Krishna and his elevation to the rank of supreme deity with the sensual worship condemned above. References to the first, that is, to his apotheosis, have been found by Professor Bhândârkar in the Mahâbhâshya, which he assigns to the second century before Christ;[1] but the latter, the Krishna-cultus proper, according to Weber, is not found before the fifth or sixth century of our era;[2] and its best authority, the Bhâgavata Purâṇa (book x.), is ascribed by Colebrooke and "many learned Hindus" to the twelfth century.[3]

In the Gopâlatâpani Upanishad, too, we find Krishna, "the beloved of the *gopîs*," set forth as the supreme deity; but this work is justly supposed by Professor Weber to be very modern,[4] and Colebrooke regarded its claim to antiquity as "particularly suspicious." His remarks on this whole question are worthy of attention. He says:—"Although the *Râmatâpanîya* be inserted in all the collections of Upanishads which I have seen; and the *Gopâlatâpanîya* appear in some, yet I am inclined to doubt their genuineness, and to suspect that they have

same. . . . The word of superior beings is true, and so also their conduct is sometimes [correct]: let a wise man observe their command, which is right. . . . Since Munis are uncontrolled and act as they please, how can there be any restraint upon him (the Supreme Deity) when he has voluntarily assumed a body?" "This passage is followed by an assurance on the part of the author of the Purâṇa that the person who listens with faith to the narrative of Krishna's sports with the cowherd's wives, and who repeats it to others, shall attain to strong devotion to that deity, and shall speedily be freed from love, that disease of the heart. A remarkable instance of homœopathic cure certainly!"—*Muir's Sanskrit Texts*, iv. 50 f. *Bhâgavata Purâṇa*, x. 33, 27–40.

[1] *Indian Antiquary*, ii. 60.

[2] *Ibid.*, p. 285.

[3] *Miscellaneous Essays*, i. 94.

[4] *History of Indian Literature*, p. 169.

been written in times modern when compared with the remainder of the Vedas. This suspicion is chiefly grounded on the opinion that the sects which now worship Râma and Krishna as incarnations of Vishnu are comparatively new. I have not found in any other part of the Vedas the least trace of such a worship. . . . According to the notions which I entertain of the real history of the Hindu religion, the worship of Râma and of Krishna by the *Vaishnavas*, and that of Mahâdeva and Bhavânî by the *Śaivas* and *Śâktas*, have been generally introduced since the persecution of the *Baudhas* and *Jainas*. . . . The overthrow of the sect of Buddha in India has not effected the full revival of the religious system inculcated in the Vedas. Most of what is there taught is now obsolete, and, in its stead, new orders of religious devotees have been instituted, and new forms of religious ceremonies have been established. Rituals founded on the *Purâṇas* and observances borrowed from a worse source, the *Tantras*, have, in a great measure, antiquated the institutions of the Vedas. In particular, the sacrificing of animals before the idols of Kâlî has superseded the less sanguinary practice of the *Yajna*; and the adoration of Râma and of Krishna has succeeded to that of the elements and planets. If this opinion be well founded, it follows that the Upanishads in question have probably been composed in later times, since the introduction of those sects which hold Râma and Gopâla in peculiar veneration."[1]

The date of that most important treatise the Bhagavad Gîtâ, in which Krishna is regarded as the Supreme, has not been determined. On account of remarkable resem-

[1] *Miscellaneous Essays*, i. 99–101.

blances in it to some of the ideas and expressions of the Bible, Dr. Lorinser, writing in 1869, asserted that it was probably indebted to the latter for them. He was of opinion that the Brahmans borrowed Christian ideas from the early Christian communities in India and applied them to Krishna.[1] The existence of a Christian Church in India in the first or second century, as maintained by Dr. Lorinser, has not, however, been satisfactorily established. According to Dr. Burnell, "the Manichæan mission to India in the third century A.D. is the only historical fact that we know of in relation to Christian missions in India before we get as low as the sixth century."[2] However this may be, the sudden appearance on the Hindu horizon of *bhakti*, as distinguished from the older *śraddhâ*,[3] is a fact the explanation of which is almost impossible if a previous contact with Christianity is denied.

Dr. Lorinser's position has been vehemently assailed by Mr. Kâshinâth Telang of Bombay, but not, in my opinion, with complete success. It has been disputed, too, by Professor Windisch of Heidelberg, who, while admitting that "some surprising parallel passages" have been adduced, considers "the immediate introduction of the Bible into the explanation of the Bhagavad Gîtâ" to be premature.[4]

Professor Weber regards Dr. Lorinser's attempt as "overdone," but adds that "he is not in principle opposed to the idea which that writer maintains."[5] Indeed this eminent scholar has declared his own belief in the indebtedness of the Krishna-cult to Christianity, as the

[1] *Indian Antiquary*, ii. 283. [2] *Ibid.*, iv. 182.
[3] Cowell's *Aphorisms of S'âṇḍilya*, p. viii.
[4] *Indian Antiquary*, iv. 79. [5] *Ibid.*

following quotation will show: "(1.) The reciprocal action and mutual influence of gnostic and Indian conceptions in the first centuries of the Christian era are evident, however difficult it may be at present to say what in each is peculiar to it or borrowed from the other. (2.) The worship of Krishna as sole god is one of the latest phases of Indian religious systems, of which there is no trace in Varâhamihira, who mentions Krishna, but only in passing. (3.) This worship of Krishna as sole god has no intelligible connection with his earlier position in the Brahmanical legends. There is a gap between the two, which apparently nothing but the supposition of an external influence can account for. (4.) The legend in the *Mahâbhârata* of Śvetadwîpa, and the revelation which is made there to Nârada by Bhagavat himself, shows that Indian tradition bore testimony to such an influence. (5.) The legends of Krishna's birth, the solemn celebration of his birthday, in the honours of which his mother, Devakí, participates, and finally his life as a herdsman, a phase the furthest removed from the original representation, can only be explained by the influence of Christian legends, which, received one after the other by individual Indians in Christian lands, were modified to suit their own ways of thought, and may also have been affected by the labours of individual Christian teachers down to the latest times."[1]

The Mahâbhârata, in which the Gîtâ lies imbedded, is the work of "widely distant periods;" and though some portion of it is said to have existed in Patanjali's time,[2] that is, in the second century before Christ, its present redaction was probably not complete until "some centuries

[1] *Indian Antiquary*, ii. 285.

[2] *Ibid.*, i. 350.

after the commencement of our era."[1] Chronology, therefore, furnishes no disproof of the theory advanced above as to the origin of Krishna-worship.

4. '*The Jyotishṭoma sacrifice.*'

This appears to have been a cycle of seven sacrifices, of which one called Agnishṭoma was the first. Dr. Haug says that in many places the term Jyotishṭoma is equivalent to Agnishṭoma, which is the model of all Soma sacrifices of one day's duration. The ceremonies connected with the Agnishṭoma sacrifice lasted for five days, but those of the first four days were merely introductory to the crowning rites of the last day, on which the squeezing, offering, and drinking of the Soma juice took place at the morning, midday, and evening libations. The Soma ceremony is said to have been the holiest rite in the whole Brahmanical service.[2]

5. '*The slaying of a Brâhman.*'

There are numerous references in Manu's code to the awfulness of this crime; and the consequences of even a common assault on his sacred person are something terrific. The following are examples :—

"That twice-born man who merely assaults a Brâhman with intent to hurt, wanders about in the hell called *Tâmisra* for a hundred years; whilst he who 'of malice aforethought' strikes him, even with a blade of grass, goes through twenty-one different births of a low order" (*Manu*, iv. 165, 166).

"A king should never slay a Brâhman, though convicted of every crime under the sun; he should expel

[1] Weber's *History of Indian Literature*, p. 188; and Muir's *Sanskrit Texts*, iv. 169.

[2] See Haug's *Aitareya Brâhmaṇa*, i. 59–63, ii. 240.

him from the country, unharmed, with all his property. There is no greater crime in the world than the slaughter of a Brâhman; a king, therefore, should not even contemplate it with his mind" (viii. 380, 381).

"The (unintentional) slayer of a Brâhman should make a hut for himself in the forest, and dwell there for twelve years for purification, living on alms, and having the head of his victim set up as a banner" (xi. 72).

"He who, with murderous intent, merely threatens a Brâhman with a stick goes to hell for a hundred years; whilst he who actually strikes him goes for a thousand years" (xi. 206).

6. '*The Sandhyâ prayers.*'

"Let him daily, after rinsing his mouth, observe the two Sandhyâs, repeating the Sâvitrî in a pure place according to rule" (*Manu*, ii. 222).

Colebrooke says: "The duty of bathing in the morning and at noon, if the man be a householder, and in the evening also, if he belong to an order of devotion, is inculcated by pronouncing the strict observance of it no less efficacious than a rigid penance in expiating sins, especially the early bath in the months of Mâgha, Phâlguna, and Kârtika; and the bath being particularly enjoined as a salutary ablution, he is permitted to bathe in his own house, but without prayers, if the weather or his own infirmities prevent his going forth; or he may abridge the ceremonies and use fewer prayers if a religious duty or urgent business require his early attendance. The regular bath consists of ablutions followed by worship and by the inaudible recitation of the Gâyatrî with the names of the worlds."[1] The sacred Gâyatrî or Sâvitrî is this:

[1] *Miscellaneous Essays*, i. 142.

'*Tat savitur vareṇyam bhargo devasya dhîmahi dhiyo yo naḥ prachodayât*,' which Colebrooke thus translates: "Let us meditate on the adorable light of the divine ruler (Savitṛi); may it guide our intellects."

7. '*The Chândrâyaṇa*.'

This, to quote from Professor Monier Williams' Dictionary, is "a religious observance or expiatory penance regulated by the moon's age. In consists in diminishing the daily consumption of food every day by one mouthful for the dark half of the month, beginning with fifteen at the full moon until the quantity is reduced to zero at the new moon, and then increasing it in like manner during the fortnight of the moon's increase." This kind is called by Manu (xi. 216, Scholium), *Pipîlikâmadhya*, 'that which has the middle thin like an ant.' If, however, the rite commences at the new moon, and goes from zero up to fifteen and then decreases again, it is called *Yavamadhya*, 'that which is thick in the middle like a barley-corn' (xi. 217). There are two other varieties called *Yati* and *Śiśu*. The former consists of eating eight mouthfuls a day at midday and fasting during the morning and evening for a whole month; the latter, of eating four mouthfuls in the morning and four in the evening every day for a month. A fifth variety, which appears to have no name, consists of eating 240 mouthfuls during the month, to be divided into daily portions at the will of the eater. Thus, as the Scholiast says, he may one day eat ten mouthfuls, another five, another sixteen, and another none at all, and so on (xi. 218–220).

8. '*The system of Śâṇḍilya*' (*Śâṇḍilyavidyâ*).

What this was is not known. It was clearly not the doctrine of faith which is set forth in the Śâṇḍilya aphorisms. See preface to Professor Cowell's translation of the latter.

9. '*Longing for emancipation.*'

The idea of *mukti* is not found in the first two divisions of the Veda, and the Śvetâśvatara is the only Upanishad in which it is fully and unmistakably developed. "The Brahmans had certainly been pondering it for some time before the rise of Buddhism. It was probably they themselves who instilled it into the mind of Śâkya. It was perhaps their own aspiration after something better than the degrading pleasures of Indra's territories that first suggested the futility of rites and ceremonies to the fertile imagination of the young prince of Kapilavastu. But it was the prince himself who appears to have imparted a coherent shape to the doctrine, which, in some of the pre-Buddhistic Upanishads, appears in a chaotic state of disconnected fragments, not unfrequently by the side of the very contrary idea of sensuous enjoyments. Śâkya appears to have first separated the two by contending that rites and ceremonies do not contribute to our highest good, and that it was *nirwâṇa* [1] alone which could secure our final escape from the miseries of sensuous life. In post-Buddhistic writings the notion of emancipation which pervades the philosophy of the Nyâya, the Sânkhya, and the Vedânta, appears in a consistent form as distinct from that of heavenly enjoyment. *Swarga* and *apawarga* are always contrasted." [2]

10. '*The qualified person.*'

The text shows that in order to qualify for initiation into the esoteric doctrines, the aspirant had to go through

[1] See this explained in Childers' *Pâli Dictionary*, s.v. *Nibbânam.*

[2] *Dialogues on Hindu Philosophy*, p. 325. See also Wilson's *Works*, ii. 113.

a long preparatory course. It may be interesting to compare with it that which the pupils of Pythagoras were required to pass through before receiving instruction in his wisdom. "For five years the novice was condemned to silence. Many relinquished the task in despair; they were unworthy of the contemplation of pure wisdom. Others, in whom the tendency to loquacity was observed to be less, had the period commuted. Various humiliations had to be endured; various experiments were made of their powers of self-denial. By these Pythagoras judged whether they were worldly-minded, or whether they were fit to be admitted into the sanctuary of science. Having purged their souls of the baser particles by purifications, sacrifices, and initiations, they were admitted to the sanctuary, where the higher part of the soul was purged by the knowledge of truth, which consists in the knowledge of immaterial and eternal things."[1]

11. '*Illusory attribution, &c.*' (*adhyâropâpavâda*).

In order to describe the pure abstraction Brahma, the teacher attributes to him, or superimposes on him, certain qualities which in reality do not belong to him, and then afterwards withdrawing them, teaches that the residuum is the undifferenced Absolute.

"When the Vedântins speak of the origin of the world, they do not believe its origin to be true. This mode of expression they call false imputation (*adhyâropa*). It consists in holding for true that which is false, in accommodation to the intelligence of the uninitiated. At a further stage of instruction, when the time has arrived for propounding the esoteric view, the false imputation is gainsaid, and this gainsaying is termed rescission[2] (*apavâda*)."

[1] Lewes' *History of Philosophy*, i. 22. [2] *Rational Refutation*, p. 209.

12. I will conclude the notes on this section with the following extract:—"If these rules of initiation be truthful, then the doctrine of one being is necessarily falsified, for they presuppose the existence of the *guru* and of all things which are necessary for the performance of the Vedic ritual; and if the rules are themselves illusory, the Vedantic initiation must itself be an illusion; and if the initiation be false, the indoctrination must be false too; for he only gets knowledge who has got an *âchârya.* The Vedânt will not allow that its grand consummation can be brought about without a qualified tutor. If there be no *âchârya,* there can be no teaching; and if the indoctrination is a delusion, the conclusion of this spiritual exercise, *i.e., mukti,* must be the grandest of delusions; and the whole system of Vedântism, all its texts and sayings, its precepts and promises, its *âchârya* and *adhikârî,* are therefore built like a house (as Râmânuja suggests) upon an imaginary mathematical line."[1]

[1] *Dialogues on Hindu Philosophy,* p. 421.

III.

Illusory attribution is the attributing to the real of that which is unreal; as a snake is imagined in a rope which is not a snake.

The '*real*' is Brahma, existent, intelligence, and joy, without a second. The '*unreal*' is the whole mass of unintelligent things, beginning with ignorance.

'*Ignorance*,' they say, is something not describable as existent or non-existent, an entity, composed of the three qualities, antagonistic to knowledge.

[Its existence is established] by one's own consciousness of being ignorant, and also by the Veda, [which speaks of it as] "the own power of God, concealed by its emanations"[1] (*Śvetâśvatara Upanishad*, i. 3).

[1] Literally, 'by its qualities,' which Śankarâchârya says means "by earth, &c., which are the products of matter" (*svagunaih prakṛitikâryabhûtaih prithivyâdibhih*).

NOTES ON SECTION III.

1. '*The real*' (*vastu*).

The characteristics of Brahma have already been considered in the opening notes, and it is in accordance with the doctrine of existences, as there explained, that Brahma is here declared to be the only reality. All else is 'unreal' (*avastu*), and imagined by ignorance. This is plainly put in the *Adhyâtma-Râmâyaṇa* (p. 477):—"The entire universe, movable and immovable, comprising bodies, intellects, and the organs, everything that is seen or heard, from Brahmâ down to a tuft of grass, is that which is called Matter (*prakṛiti*), is that which is known as Illusion."

The phenomenal is got rid of in this simple way, by quietly ignoring the evidence of the senses; but the non-duality thus established is purely imaginary. For "even appearances or illusions are phenomena which require to be explained, and they cannot be explained on the hypothesis of absolute unity. They imply that besides the absolute being there are *minds* which can be haunted by appearances, and which can be deluded into believing that these appearances are realities."[1]

It has been already stated that the teaching of the earlier Upanishads was a *pariṇâmavâda*, not a *mâyâvâda* or *vivarttavâda*. Whence, then, did this theory of the unreality of all things arise? The most probable answer is, that it was adopted from the Buddhists, the great supporters of Idealism. This was the opinion of Vijnâna

[1] *Anti-Theistic Theories*, p. 419.

Bhikshu, the learned commentator on the Śankhya philosophy, who flourished about 300 years ago,[1] and who wrote of the "quasi-Vedantins" of his time as "upstart disguised Buddhists, advocates of the theory of Mâyâ," and quoted a passage from the Padma Purâṇa[2] where the doctrine of Mâyâ is also stigmatised as nothing but disguised Buddhism.[3] The Śvetâśvatara is said to be the only Upanishad in which the illusory nature of phenomena is plainly taught, and that tract is evidently post-Buddhistic. In the preface to his translation of it, Dr. Roer says that it "does not belong to the series of the more ancient Upanishads, or of those which preceded the foundation of the philosophical systems; for it shows, in many passages, an acquaintance with them, introduces the Vedânta, Sânkhya, and Yoga by their very names—mentions the reputed founder of the Sânkhya, Kapila, and appears even to refer to doctrines which have been always considered as heterodox. . . . As the mythological views of the Śvetâśvatara are those of a later time, when the worship of Śiva and of the divine Śaktis or energies had gained ground, in contradistinction to the ancient Upanishads, where only the gods of the Vedas are introduced, so also its philosophical doctrine refers to a more modern period." In his opinion, it was composed not very long before the time of Śankarâchârya, who is thought to have flourished in the eighth century of our era.[4]

2. '*Ignorance*' (*ajnâna*).

This is synonymous with Nescience (*avidyâ*) and Illusion

[1] Preface to Hall's *Sânkhya Sâra*, p. 37 (*note*).

[2] This work is supposed by Professor H. H. Wilson to have been composed, in part, in the twelfth century. *Vishnu Purâṇa*, vol. i. p. xxxiv.

[3] *Dialogues on Hindu Philosophy*, pp. 309–313. *Sânkhya-pravachara-bhâshya*, p. 29.

[4] Colebrooke's *Essays*, i. 357.

(*mâyâ*), and though called the material cause of the universe, nevertheless heads the list of unrealities! Indeed it has been said that "the tenet of the falseness of Ignorance is the very keystone of the Vedânta!"[1] Its properties are the following:—

(a.) '*Not describable as existent or non-existent.*'

If allowed to have true existence, dualism of cause ensues; and if it be said to be non-existent, it falls into the same category as a hare's horn, the son of a barren woman, and such like absolute nonentities, and no causation could then be attributed to it. So, to avoid the dilemma, it is said to be neither the one nor the other. Howbeit it is acknowledged to have a practical existence, and to have been eternally associated with Brahma;[2] and, as a matter of fact, Brahma and Mâyâ are the exact counterpart of the Purusha and Prakṛiti of the Sânkhya, which is a professedly dualistic system.

A native writer speaks of Illusion as "the inscrutable principle regulating the universe of phenomena, or rather the world itself regarded as ultimately inconceivable;"[3] and, elsewhere, as "the mystery by which the absolute Brahma brings himself into relation to the universe;"[4] but he allows that, after all, this is rather a confession of the mystery than a solution of it. By Śankarâchârya it is defined as "the aggregate of all powers, causes, and effects." But a principle or power producing such palpable results as the universe, &c., must have a very real existence, however 'inscrutable' it may be; and the definition of the text is absolute nonsense. The philo-

[1] *Rational Refutation*, p. 193. [2] *Ibid.*, p. 35 (*note*).

[3] *The Pandit* (*new series*), iii. 506.

[4] *Journal of R. A. S.* (*new series*), x. 38.

sopher Kapila discusses this point in some of the aphorisms of his first book: "Not from Ignorance too [does the soul's bondage, as the Vedântists hold, arise], because that which is not a reality is not adapted to binding. If it [Ignorance] *be* [asserted by you to be] a reality, then there is an abandonment of the [Vedantic] tenet. And [if you assume Ignorance to be a reality, then] there would be a *duality* through [there being] something of a different kind [from soul,—which you asserters of *non-duality* cannot contemplate allowing]. If [the Vedântin alleges, regarding Ignorance, that] it is in the shape of both these opposites, [we say] no, because no such thing is known [as is at once real and unreal]. [Possibly the Vedântin may remonstrate], '*We* are not asserters of any six categories like the Vaiśeshikas and others [—like the Vaiśeshikas who arrange all things under six heads, and the Naiyâyikas who arrange them under sixteen;—'therefore we hold that there *is* such a thing as Ignorance, which is at once real and unreal, or (if you prefer it) which differs at once from the real and unreal, because this is established by proofs,' scriptural or otherwise, which are satisfactory to *us*, although they may not comply with all the technical requisitions of Gautama's scheme of argumentative exposition. To which we reply], Even although this be not compulsory [that the categories be reckoned six or sixteen], there is no acceptance of the inconsistent, else we come to the level of children, madmen, and the like."[1]

(b.) '*An entity*' (*bhâvarûpa*).

This is laid down in opposition to the notion of the

[1] *Sânkhya Aphorisms*, translated by Dr. Ballantyne, pp. 6–8.

logicians that *ajnâna*, 'not-knowledge,' is merely the equivalent of *jnânâbhâva*, 'absence of knowledge.'

(c.) *'Antagonistic to knowledge'* (*jnânavirodhi*).

This may possibly mean, 'whose foe is knowledge,' that is, 'which is capable of being destroyed by knowledge.' A man might argue, says the commentator, that Ignorance being, according to the Veda, 'unborn,' spread out everywhere like the ether, and having the semblance of reality, deliverance from its power and from transmigration is impossible; but it is not so, for notwithstanding the power of Ignorance, it nevertheless yields to the cognition of Brahma, as the darkness flees before the light. There can be no doubt, from what has been so far asserted of Ignorance, that the logicians have rightly defined it as 'absence of apprehension,' and that it is also 'misapprehension.' For further on we shall find two powers attributed to Ignorance, namely, those of 'concealment' (*âvaraṇa*) and 'projection' (*vikshepa*), which are nothing else than 'absence of apprehension,' and 'misapprehension,' respectively.[1]

(d.) *'Composed of the three qualities'* (*trigunâtmaka*).

This is stated, too, in Bhagavad Gîtâ, vii. 14: "Inasmuch as this divine Mâyâ of mine, composed of the qualities, is hard to be surmounted, none but those who resort to me cross over it." The *Prakṛiti*, that is, 'Nature' or 'Matter,' of the Sânkhya has been thus described:—"Nature is unintelligent substance, and is the material cause of the world. It consists of goodness, passion, and darkness in equal proportions. And here it should be borne in mind that it is not the goodness, passion, and darkness, popularly reckoned qualities or particular states

[1] *Rational Refutation*, p. 248.

of the soul, that are intended in the Sânkhya. In it they are *unintelligent substances.* Otherwise, how could they be the material cause of earth and like gross things?"[1]

Every word of this applies to the Vedantic 'Ignorance' or 'Illusion,' which, in the Śvetâśvatara Upanishad (iv. 10) is called Prakṛiti, or matter, and which is held to be the material cause of the world.

How this fact is to be reconciled with the previous portions of the definition is for the Vedantist to explain, if he can!

[1] *Rational Refutation*, p. 42.

IV.

THIS Ignorance is treated as one or as many, according as it is regarded as a collective or distributive aggregate. Just as, when regarding a collection of trees as a whole, we speak of them as one thing, namely, a forest; or as, when regarding a collection of waters as a whole we call them a lake, so when we look at the aggregate of the ignorances residing in individual souls and seeming to be manifold, we regard them as one. As it is said in the Veda, "[The one, unborn, individual soul, approaches] the one, unborn (Nature)" (*Śvetâśvatara Upanishad*, iv. 5).

This collective aggregate [of Ignorances], having as its associate that which is most excellent,[1] abounds in pure goodness. Intelligence [2] associated with it, having the qualities of omniscience, omnipotence, and universal control, real and unreal, imperceptible, the internal ruler and the cause of the world, is called Îśwara.

[1] Namely, the *whole* of that portion of Brahma which is associated with ignorance.

[2] *Chaitanya* or *Brahma*.

Omniscience is attributed to him as the illuminator of the whole of Ignorance. As the Veda says, "Who knows all [generally], who knows everything [particularly]" (*Muṇḍaka*, i. 1, 9).

This totality [of Ignorance], being the cause of all things, is Îśwara's causal body. It is also called 'the sheath of bliss,' because it is replete with bliss, and envelops all things like a sheath; and 'dreamless sleep,' because everything reposes in it,—on which account it is also regarded as the scene of the dissolution of all subtile and gross bodies.

As, when regarding a forest as a distributive aggregate composed of trees, there is a perception of its manifoldness, which is also perceived in the case of a lake regarded as a distributive aggregate of waters,—so, when viewing Ignorance distributively, we perceive it to be multiplex. As the Veda says, "Indra, by his supernatural powers, appears multiform" (*Rig-Veda*, 6. 47. 18).

Thus, then, a thing is regarded as a collective or distributive aggregate according as it is viewed as a whole or as a collection of parts.

Distributive ignorance, having a humble [1] associate, abounds in impure goodness. Intelligence

[1] Namely, that small underlying portion of Brahma which forms the individual soul.

associated with it, having the qualities of parviscience and parvipotence, is called *Prâjna*.[1] The smallness of its intelligence is owing to its being the illuminator of one Ignorance only. It has not the power of enlightening much, because its associate is not clear.

This [distributive Ignorance] is the individual's causal body, because it is the cause of the making of 'I,' &c. It is also called 'the sheath of bliss,' because it abounds in bliss and covers like a sheath; and 'dreamless sleep,' because all things repose in it,—on which account it is said to be the scene of the dissolution of the subtile and gross body.

Both *Îśwara* and *Prâjna* experience bliss by means of the very subtile modifications of Ignorance lighted up by Intelligence. As the Veda says, "Prâjna, whose sole inlet is the intellect, enjoys bliss" (*Mâṇḍukya Upanishad*, 5).

And, as is proved by the experience of one who on rising says, "I slept pleasantly, I was conscious of nothing."

Between these two, the collective and distri-

[1] This word is here made to mean a 'limited intelligence,' such as each individual is. In the sixth verse of the Mâṇḍukya Upanishad, however, it is described as "almighty, omniscient, &c.;" and Śankarâchârya defines *Prâjna* as meaning one who has knowledge of the past and future, and of all objects.

butive aggregates [of Ignorance], there is no difference; just as there is none between a forest and its trees, or between a lake and its waters.

Nor is there any difference between Îśwara and Prâjna, who are associated respectively with these [collective and distributive aggregates of Ignorance]; just as there is none between the ether appropriated [*i.e.*, the space occupied] by the forest and that appropriated by the trees composing it,—or between the sky reflected in the lake, and that reflected in its waters. As it is said in the Veda, "This is the lord of all, omniscient, the internal ruler, the source of all, for it is the source and reabsorbent of all creatures"[1] (*Mâṇḍukya Upanishad*, 6).

As there is an unappropriated ether, the source of that appropriated by a forest or by its trees, and of that reflected in a lake or its waters—so too, there is Intelligence which is not associated with Ignorance, the source of these two Ignorance-associated Intelligences [Îśwara and Prâjna]. It is called *the Fourth.* As it is said in the Veda, "They consider that calm, blissful, secondless one to be the Fourth. That is Soul,—that is to be known" (*Mâṇḍukya*, 7).

[1] This is said of *Prâjna.*

This one, the Fourth, pure intelligence, when not discerned as separate from Ignorance, and Intelligence associated with it, like a red-hot iron ball [viewed without discriminating between the iron and the fire], is the literal meaning of the great sentence ['That art Thou']; but when discerned as separate, it is the meaning that is *indicated.*

This Ignorance has two powers, namely, that of (*a*) *envelopment* (or *concealment*), and of (*b*) *projection.*

The power of *envelopment* is such that, just as even a small cloud, by obscuring the beholder's path of vision, seems to overspread the sun's disc, which is many leagues in extent,—so Ignorance, though limited, veiling the understanding of the beholder, seems to cover up Soul, which is unlimited, and unconnected with the universe. As it has been said, "As he whose eye is covered by a cloud, thinks in his delusion that the sun is clouded and has lost its light,—so that Soul which seems bound to him whose mind's eye is blind,—that Soul, essentially eternal perception, am I."[1]

Soul, covered up by this [enveloping power],

[1] *Hastâmalaka*, 12.

appears to be an agent and a patient, and to experience pleasure, pain, and other mundane conditions; just as a rope, covered by ignorance as to its real nature, appears to be a snake.

The power of *projection* is such, that, just as ignorance regarding a rope, by its own power raises up the form of a snake, &c., on the rope which is covered by it,—so Ignorance too, by its own power, raises up, on Soul which is covered by it, ether and the whole universe. As it has been said, "The projective power [of Ignorance] can create the world, beginning with subtile bodies, and ending with the terrene orb."[1]

Intelligence, associated with Ignorance possessed of these two powers, is, when itself is chiefly considered, the efficient cause; and when its associate is chiefly considered, is the material cause. Just as a spider, when itself is chiefly considered, is the efficient cause of its web, the effect,—and when its body is chiefly considered, is the material cause of it.

[1] *Vâkyasudhâ*, v. 13.

NOTES ON SECTION IV.

In the foregoing pages, two eternal entities have been described, namely, Brahma and Ignorance. These two have been united from everlasting, and the first product of their union is Îśwara or God. It should be very distinctly understood that God—"the highest of manifestations in the world of unreality"[1]—is the collective aggregate of all animated things, from the highest deity down to a blade of grass, just as a forest is a collective aggregate of trees.

This, to any ordinary mind, is tantamount to saying that there is no personal God at all; for how can it be supposed that this aggregate of sentiencies has, or has ever had, any power of united action, so as to constitute it a personal Being? Yet, after describing God as identical with the aggregate of individual sentiencies, apart from which he can have no more existence than a forest can have apart from the trees which compose it, the text proceeds to treat him as a personal Being, endowed with the qualities of omniscience, &c., and bearing rule over individual souls!

The attributes assigned to him are thus explained by the commentator. His '*omniscience*' is merely his being a witness of the whole universe, animate and inanimate; or, as the text puts it, He is omniscient as being the illuminator of the whole body of illusion. He is called '*Îśwara,*' because he presides over individual souls, and

[1] *Calcutta Review*, 1878, p. 314. See also *Rational Refutation*, p. 211.

allots rewards according to their works. How this aggregate of individual souls is to preside over itself, and reward each soul included in it according to its works, it is impossible to say;[1] but his functions in this capacity ought to be a sinecure, inasmuch as it is strongly insisted upon that works, whether good or bad, are followed by an exactly proportioned measure of reward or punishment, without the intervention of anybody. He is the '*controller*' in the sense of being the mover or impeller of souls; and the '*internal ruler*' as dwelling in the heart of each, and restraining the intellect. He is the '*cause of the world*,' not as its creator, but as the seat of the evolution of that illusory effect. Indeed, it would be inconsistent to speak of a creator of a world which has no greater reality than belongs to things seen in a dream!

2. '*Îśwara's causal body.*'

As Illusion overlying Brahma is the cause of the production of all things, it is called Îśwara's causal or all-originating body. From it originate the super-sensible and sensible elements, then subtile bodies, and, lastly, gross bodies. These envelop transmigrating souls like sheaths, which have to be successively stripped off to reach pure Brahma.

3. '*Dreamless sleep.*'

There are said to be three states of the soul in respect of the body, viz., waking, dreaming, and dreamless sleep. Brahma is described as 'the fourth' state. "When a man with all his wits about him is wide awake, he is regarded as being furthest removed from the state in which he ought to be,—he being then enveloped in the densest in-

[1] One might as well assert the possibility of a man's sitting on his own shoulders!

vestment of Ignorance. When he falls asleep and dreams, he is considered to have shuffled off his outermost coil; and therefore a dream is spoken of as the scene of the dissolution of the totality of the gross. The objects viewed in dreams are regarded as 'subtile.' When a man sleeps so soundly that he has no dream, he is regarded as having got rid not only of his 'gross body' but also of his 'subtile body;' hence profound and dreamless sleep is spoken of as the 'scene of the dissolution both of the gross and of the subtile body.' But although, in profound sleep, a man has got rid of all the *developments* of Ignorance, yet he is still wrapped in Ignorance itself, and this must be got rid of. He must not, like the sleeper who 'slept pleasantly and knew nothing,' 'enjoy blessedness by means of the very subtile modifications of Ignorance illuminated by Intellect,' but he must become Intellect simply—identical with Blessedness. To this absolute Unity is given the name of 'the Fourth.'"[1]

The following remarks of Colebrooke's are of interest in this connection:—"In profound sleep the soul is absent, having retired by the channel of the arteries, and being as it were enfolded in the supreme deity. It is not, however, blended with the divine essence, as a drop of water fallen into a lake when it becomes undistinguishable; but, on the contrary, the soul continues discriminate, and returns unchanged to the body which it animates while awake. Swoon or stupor is intermediate between sleep and death. During insensibility produced by accident or disease, there is, as in profound sleep and lethargy, a temporary absence of the soul. In death it has absolutely quitted its gross corporeal frame."[2]

[1] Dr. Ballantyne's *Lecture on the Vedânta*, para. 152 (f).

[2] Colebrooke's *Essays*, i. 398.

V.

From Intelligence associated with Ignorance attended by its projective power, in which the quality of insensibility (*tamas*) abounds, proceeds ether,—from ether, air,—from air, heat,—from heat, water,—and from water, earth. As the Veda says, "From this, from this same Self, was the ether produced" (*Taittirîya Upanishad*, 2. 1). The prevalence of insensibility in the cause of these elements is inferred from observing the excess of inanimateness which is in them.[1]

Then, in those elements, ether and the rest, arise the qualities pleasure, pain, and insensibility, in the proportion in which they exist in their cause. These are what are termed the subtile elements, the rudimentary elements, the non-quintuplicated [lit. 'not become the five,' by combination].

From them spring the subtile bodies and the gross elements.

1 "The elements being unenlightened by Intellect, which they quite obscure."—Ballantyne's *Lecture on the Vedânta.*

The '*subtile bodies*' are the distinguishing [or evidentiary] bodies, consisting of seventeen members.

The '*members*' are the five organs of sense, mind, and intellect, the five organs of action, and the five vital airs.

The '*organs of sense*' are the ear, skin, eye, tongue, and nose. These arise separately, in order, from the unmingled pleasure-portions of ether and the rest.[1]

'*Intellect*' is the modification of the internal organ which is characterised by certitude; '*mind*' is the modification characterised by resolution and irresolution; in these two are included thinking and egoism.

'*Thinking*' is that affection of the internal organ characterised by investigation; '*egoism*' is the affection characterised by self-consciousness. These two arise from the *united* pleasure-endowed portions of ether and the others. That they are the effect of the pleasure-portions of the elements is inferred from their being luminous.

This intellect, together with the organs of sense, forms the cognitional sheath (*vijnânamayakośa*).

[1] That is to say, from ether, the characteristic of which is sound, came the ear,—from air, of which mobility is the characteristic, and in which sound and feel are sensible, came the sense of touch, and so on.

This one, which fancies itself to be an agent and a patient, and passes to and fro between this and the other world [*i.e.*, a transmigrating soul], is called the conventional[1] soul.

The mind, together with the organs of action, form the mental [or sensorial] sheath (*manomayakośa*).

The '*organs of action*' are the mouth, hand, foot, anus, and generative organ. These arise, separately, in order, from the unmixed pain-portions of the elements [which are characterised by *activity*].

The '*vital airs*' are respiration (*prâṇa*), inspiration (*apâna*), flatuousness (*vyâna*), expiration (*udâna*), and digestion (*samâna*). '*Respiration*' has an upward motion, and abides in the extremity of the nose; '*inspiration*' has a downward course, and abides in the anus, &c.; '*flatuousness*' moves in all directions, and pervades the whole body; '*expiration*' belongs to the throat, has an upward course, and is the ascending air; '*digestion*' is the assimilation of solid and liquid food on its reaching the stomach.

[1] "There can be no such thing as a substance existing *conventionally* but not *really*. Things there may be, existing in the opinions of men or implied in their conduct, but if we deny their reality, we can only mean that they are mere fancies, and therefore not actually existing substances. . . . In fact, conventional, as opposed to real, can only mean imaginary, in other words, false."—*Dialogues*, p. 394.

'*Assimilation*' is the causing of digestion, and the production of juice, blood, semen, excrement, &c.

Some persons [followers of Kapila] say that there are five other airs, named Nâga, Kûrma, Kṛikara, Devadatta, and Dhananjaya.

'*Nâga*' is that which causes eructation; '*kûrma*' is that which causes the opening and closing of the eyes; '*kṛikara*' causes hunger, and '*devadatta*' yawning; and '*dhananjaya*'[1] is the nourisher.

But others [the Vedântins] say that there are five only, as these are included in the previous five, respiration and the rest.

This set of five vital airs arises from the united pain-portions of the elements, ether and the others. The five, together with the organs of action, form the respiratory sheath. Its being a product of the pain-portions of the elements, is inferred from its being endowed with activity [the characteristic of the '*rajoguna*'].

Of these sheaths, 'the intellectual,' being endowed with the faculty of knowing, is an agent;

[1] This air continues in the body even after death, says the scholiast, quoting from some author: "*na jahâti mṛitañchâpi sarvavyâpî dhananjayah!*"

the 'mental,' having the faculty of desire, is an instrument; and the 'respiratory,' having the faculty of activity, is an effect. This division is in accord with the capabilities of each. These three sheaths together constitute the subtile frame.[1]

Here, too, the totality of the subtile bodies, as the seat of one intellect [*i.e.*, Sûtrâtmâ's], is a collective aggregate like the forest or the lake; or, as the seat of many intellects [viz., those of individual souls], is a distributive aggregate, like the forest trees or the lake-waters.

Intelligence associated with the collective aggregate [of subtile bodies] is called Sûtrâtmâ [Thread-soul], Hiraṇyagarbha, or Prâṇa, because it passes as a thread through all [the subtile frames], and on account of the conceit that it is the five uncompounded elements possessing the faculties of knowing, desire, and activity [*i.e.*, that it is the subtile body itself].

This aggregate, because it is more subtile than the gross organisms, is called His subtile body, consisting of the three sheaths, 'the intellectual' and the others; and because it consists of the [continuance of the] waking thoughts, it is called a

[1] It attends the soul in its transmigrations.

dream, and is therefore said to be the scene of the dissolution of the gross.[1]

Intelligence associated with the distributive aggregate of subtile organisms is *Taijasa* (the brilliant), because it has the luminous internal organ as its associate.

This distributive aggregate, too, being more subtile than the gross organisms, is called his subtile frame, comprising the three sheaths beginning with 'the intellectual;' and it is said to be a dream because it is made up of the [continuance of the] waking thoughts, on which account it is called the scene of the dissolution of the gross organisms.

These two, the Thread-soul [Sûtrâtmâ] and Taijasa, by means of the subtile modifications of the mind, have experience of subtile objects. As it is said in the Veda, "Taijasa has fruition of the supersensible" (*Mâṇḍukya*, 4).

There is no difference between the collective and distributive aggregates of the subtile frames, or between Sûtrâtmâ and Taijasa, who are asso-

[1] "For, in a dream, the sight of trees and rivers, and the sound of voices, &c., are present to us, without the actual things called trees, &c., being present at all. To the dreamer, the whole external world is as it were not,—and, in the opinion of the Vedântin, to the dreamer it really *is* not."—*Lecture on the Vedânta.*

ciated with them,—just as there is none between the forest and its trees, or between the space occupied by each,—or between the lake and its waters, and the sky reflected in each.

Thus were the subtile organisms produced.

The gross elements are those that have been made by combining the five [subtile elements]. Quintuplication is on this wise. After dividing each of the five subtile elements, ether and the rest, into two equal parts, and then subdividing each of the first five of the ten moieties into four equal parts, mix those four parts with the others, leaving the [undivided] second moiety of each. As it has been said, "After dividing each into two parts, and the first halves again into four parts, by uniting the latter to the second half of each, each contains the five"[1] (*Panchadaśî*, i. 27).

It must not be supposed that there is no authority for this, for from the Vedic passage regarding the combination of three things,[2] the combination of five is implied. Though the five alike contain

[1] That is, "the particles of the several elements, being divisible, are, in the first place, split into moieties; whereof one is subdivided into quarters, and the remaining moiety combines with one part (a quarter of a moiety) from each of the four others."—Colebrooke's *Essays*, i. 396. Each of the five elements thus contains a moiety of itself and an eighth of each of the others.

[2] *Chhândogya Upanishad*, 6. 3. 3.

the five, the name 'ether' and the rest are still applicable[1] to them, in accordance with the saying, "For the sake of distinction, one has this name, and another that" (*Vedânta Sûtras*, 2. 4. 22). Then, in ether sound is manifested,—in air, sound and touch,—in heat, sound, touch, and form,—in water, sound, touch, form, and taste,—in earth, sound, touch, form, taste, and smell.

From these quintuplicated elements spring, one above the other, the worlds Bhûr, Bhuvar, Swar, Mahar, Janas, Tapas, and Satya; and, one below the other, the nether worlds called Atala, Vitala, Sutala, Rasâtala, Talâtala, Mahâtala, and Pâtâla;[2] —Brahmâ's egg;—the four kinds of gross bodies included in it; and food and drink.

'*The four kinds of gross bodies*' are the viviparous, the oviparous, the moisture-engendered, and the germinating.

The viviparous are those produced from the womb, as men and animals; *the oviparous* are those born from eggs, as birds and snakes; *the moisture-engendered* are those which spring from

[1] The name 'ether' is suitable to the first because 'ether' largely predominates in it, and so with the other four.

[2] For an account of these upper and lower regions, see Wilson's *Vishnu Purâṇa*, ii. 209, 225.

moisture, as lice and gnats; *the germinating* are those which shoot up from the ground, as creepers and trees.

In this case, too, the fourfold gross body, viewed as the seat of one [collective] intellect or of many [individual] intellects, is a collective aggregate like a forest or a lake, or a distributive aggregate like the forest-trees or the lake-waters.

Intelligence associated with the collective aggregate is called Vaiśwânara [the spirit of humanity] or Virâṭ;[1] [the former] because of the conceit that it is in the whole of humanity, and [the latter] because it appears in various forms.[2]

This collective aggregate is his gross body. It is called 'the nutrimentitious sheath,' on account of the changes of food [which go on within it and build it up], and it is said to be awake, because it is the scene of the fruition of the gross.

Intelligence associated with the distributive aggregate is called Viśwa, because, without abandoning the conceit of the subtile body, it enters into all gross bodies.

[1] Compare *Manu*, i. 32, 33, and *Sanskrit Texts*, v. 369.

[2] I have followed the scholiast, who says, *Sarvaprâṇinikâyeshvaham ityabhimânatwâd vaiśwânaratwam; nânâprakâreṇa prakâśamânatwâchcha vairâjatwam labhate ityarthah.* Ballantyne's rendering of the last clause is, "Because it rules over the various kinds [of bodies]."

This distributive aggregate is his gross body, and is called the nutrimentitious sheath on account of the changes of food [which go on within it and build it up]. It is also said to be awake because it is the seat of the fruition of the gross.

Viśwa and Vaiśwânara have experience of all gross objects; that is, by means of the ear and the rest of the five organs of sense, which are controlled by the quarters, wind, the sun, Varuna, and the Aświns respectively, [they have experience of] sound, sensation, form, taste, and smell;—by means of the mouth and the rest of the five organs of action, which are controlled by Agni, Indra, Upendra, Yama, and Prajâpati respectively, [they have experience of] speaking, taking, walking, evacuation, and sensual delights; and by means of the four internal organs, named mind, intellect, egoïsm, and thinking, which are controlled by the moon, Brahmâ, Śiva, and Vishnu respectively, [they have experience of] doubting, certitude, egoising, and thought. As it is said in the Veda, ["The first quarter is Vaiśwânara], who is in the waking state, and has cognition of externals" (*Mânḍukya Upanishad*, 3).

Here, too, as in the former cases, there is no

difference between the distributive and collective aggregates of gross organisms, or between Viśwa and Vaiśwânara who are associated with them; just as there is none between a forest and its trees, or between the spaces occupied by them,—or between a lake and its waters, or between the sky reflected in them.

In this way is the gross produced from the five elements quintuplicated.

NOTES ON SECTION V.

1. Recapitulating, then, Brahma is illusorily associated with three kinds of bodies :—

Firstly, with a causal body, composed of Ignorance or Illusion, which, in the aggregate, is Îśwara or God, and, distributively, individual souls or Prâjna. It is likened to a state of dreamless sleep.

Secondly, with a subtile body, composed of the five organs of sense and of action, mind, intellect, and the five vital airs, seventeen in all. This, in the aggregate, is called Hiraṇyagarbha, or the Thread-soul, and, in the distributed state, Taijasa. It is likened to a state of dream.

Thirdly, with a gross body composed of the compounded elements. Viewed in the aggregate, it is called Vaiśwânara, and distributively, Viśwa. It is likened to the waking state.

A fourth state is that of the unassociated pure Brahma, who is technically styled 'The Fourth.'

2. Mind, intellect, egoism and thinking, which, on page 66, are styled 'internal organs,' are, collectively, 'the internal organ.' See note on page 5.

VI.

THE aggregate of all these expanses of gross, subtile, and causal bodies is one vast expanse; just as the aggregate of a number of minor [or included] forests is one large forest, or that of a number of minor [or included] bodies of water is one large body.

Intelligence associated with it, from Viśwa and Vaiśwânara up to Îśwara, is one only; just as the space occupied by the various included forests is one, or as the sky reflected in the various included bodies of water is one.

Unassociated Intelligence not seen to be distinct from the great expanse and the Intelligence associated with it, like a heated ball of iron, [in which the iron and the fire are not discriminated,] is the literal [or primary] meaning of the great sentence, "Truly all this is Brahma;" but when seen as distinct, it is what is indicated by that sentence.

Thus 'illusory attribution,' or the superimposing

of the unreal upon the Real, has been set forth in general terms. But now, the particular way in which one man imposes this and another that upon the all-pervading [individuated] self is to be declared.

For example, the very illiterate man says that his son is his self; on account of the text of the Veda [*cf. Śatapatha Brâhmaṇa,* 14. 9. 4. 26], "Self is born as a son;" and because he sees that he has the same love for his son as for himself; and because he finds that if it is well or ill with his son, it is well or ill with himself.

A Chârvâka says that the gross body is his self; on account of the text of the Veda [*Taittirîya Upanishad,* 2. 1], "This is man as made up of the extract of food;" and because he sees that a man leaving his own son [to burn], departs himself from a burning house; and because of the experience, "*I* am fat," "*I* am lean."

Another Chârvâka says that the organs of sense are his self; on account of the text of the Veda (*Chhândogya Upanishad,* v. 1. 7), "They, the organs of sense (*prâṇâh*), went to Prajâpati and said, ['Lord, which of us is the chief?' He said unto them, 'He is chief among you whose departure makes the body seem worthless'];" and because in the absence of the organs of sense the functions of the body cease; and because of the experience, "*I* am blind of one eye," "*I* am deaf."

Another Chârvâka says that the vital airs are his self; on account of the text of the Veda (*Taittirîya Upanishad,* 2. 2), "There is another, an inner self, made of the vital airs;" and because in the absence of the vital airs the organs of sense are inactive; and because of the experience, "*I* am hungry," "*I* am thirsty."

Another Chârvâka says that the mind is his self; on account of the text of the Veda (*Taittirîya Upanishad,* 2. 3), "There is another, an inner self, made of the mind;" and because when the mind sleeps the vital airs cease to be; and because of the experience, "*I* resolve," "*I* doubt."

A Bauddha says that intellect is his self; on account of the text of the Veda (*Taittirîya,* 2. 4), "There is another, an inner self, made up of cognition;" and because, in the absence of an agent, an instrument is powerless; and because of the experience, "*I* am an agent," "*I* am a patient."

The Prâbhâkara and the Târkika say that ignorance is their self; on account of the text of the Veda (*Taittirîya,* 2. 5), "There is another, an inner self, made up of bliss;" and because, during sleep, intellect and the rest are merged in ignorance; and because of the experience, "*I* am ignorant."

The Bhâṭṭa says that Intelligence associated with ignorance is his self; on account of the text of the Veda (*Mânḍukya Upanishad*, 5), "Self is a mass of knowledge, and comprised of bliss;" and because during sleep there are both the light [of intelligence] and the darkness [of ignorance[1]]; and because of the experience, "Myself I know not."

Another Bauddha says that nihility is his self; on account of the text of the Veda, "In the beginning, this was a mere nonentity;" and because during sleep everything disappears; and because of the experience of the man who has just awoke from sleep,—an experience in the shape of a reflection on his own non-existence,—when he says, "I slept—during sleep, *I* was not."

That these, beginning with 'son' and ending with 'nihility,' have not the nature of self, is now declared. Seeing that, in the fallacies based on

[1] "For, as the commentator says, referring to the sentence 'I slept pleasantly—I was aware of nothing,' if there were not light or knowledge in the soul, how could the sleeper have known that his sleep was pleasant? And if there were not the absence of light or knowledge, how could he say 'I was aware of nothing'?"—Ballantyne's *Lecture on the Vedanta.*

Vedic texts, arguments, and personal experience, brought forward by the 'very illiterate man' and the other speakers, each succeeding fallacy refutes the notion of self put forth in that preceding it, it is clear that 'son' and the rest are not the self.

Moreover, from the opposite statements of other strong Vedic texts to the effect that the all-pervading [individuated] self is not gross, not the eye, not the vital airs, not the mind, not an agent, but intelligence, pure intelligence, and existent,—from the transitory character, as of a jar, of the insentient objects beginning with 'son' and ending with 'nihility,' which owe their visibility to Intelligence, —from the force of the experience of the wise, viz., 'I am Brahma,'—and also from the fact that the fallacies based on this and that Vedic passage, argument, and personal experience have been refuted,—each of those from 'son' down to 'nihility' is assuredly not the self.

Therefore, all-pervading [individuated] Intelligence alone, the illuminator of each of those [son and the rest], whose nature is eternal, pure, intelligent, free and true, is the true self—such is the experience of those who know the Vedânta.

NOTES ON SECTION VI.

1. The *Chârvâkas,* otherwise called *Śûnyavâdins* or *Lokâyatikas,* were one of the ancient heretical sects of Hindus. Professor Wilson says of them (*Works,* ii. 87) that they " condemned all ceremonial rites, ridiculed even the Śrâddha, and called the authors of the Vedas fools, knaves, and buffoons." He says too that they were " named from one of their teachers, the Muni Chârvâka. . . . The appellation Śûnyavâdî implies the asserter of the unreality and emptiness of the universe; and another designation, Lokâyata, expresses their adoption of the tenet, that this being is the *Be-all* of existence; they were, in short, the advocates of materialism and atheism " (*Works,* i. 22). Colebrooke, too, calls their doctrine " undisguised materialism." According to this scholar, their principal tenets were, (*a*) the identity of the soul with the body,—(*b*) the rejection of *âkâśa* as an element,—and (*c*) the acknowledgment of perception alone as a means of proof. Their doctrines are explained in the first chapter of the *Sarvadarśanasangraha,* which has been translated by Professor Cowell.[1]

2. The *Bauddhas,* or followers of Buddha, are said by Brahmanical controversialists to have been divided into

[1] *Vide* pamphlet entitled " *The Chârvâka System of Philosophy.*"—The term *Lokâyata,* or *Lokâyatika,* is here explained to be that applied to men who held the opinion, 'widely prevalent in the world' (*lokeshu âyatam vistîrṇam yanmatam asti*), that wealth and desire are the only ends of man, and that there is no future world.

four sects, styled *Mâdhyamikas, Yogâchâras, Sautrântikas,* and *Vaibhâshikas.* Those referred to in the text would be the first two, the former of whom are said to have maintained that all is void, and the latter that all is void but intelligence. Possibly these four schools did at one time exist amongst the Indian Buddhists; but it is difficult to understand how they could have held the views ascribed to them in the text. For one of the cardinal doctrines of Buddhism is that *there is no self.* One of the best authorities on Southern Buddhist teaching thus wrote:—"The idea of the Brahmans is, that there is a supreme existence, *paramâtmâ,* from which each individual existence has derived its being, but that this separate existence is an illusion; and that the grand object of man is to effect the destruction of the cause of seeming separation, and to secure the reunion of the derived and the underived, the conditioned and the unconditioned. But Buddha repeatedly, by an exhaustive variation of argument, denies that there is any self or ego. Again and again, he runs over the components and essentialities of being, enumerating with tedious minuteness the classifications into which they may be divided, in order to convince his followers that, in whatever way these constituents may be placed, or however they may be arranged, there can be found in them no self."[1] How then could the Buddhists referred to in the text have held 'nihility' or 'intelligence' to be *self?*

3. The *Prâbhâkaras* were the followers of Prabhâkara, the well-known scholiast of the Pûrva-Mimânsâ; the

[1] Hardy's *Legends and Theories of the Buddhists,* p. 171. See also this author's *Manual of Buddhism,* p. 405; and Rhys Davids' *Buddhism,* pp. 90–99.

Târkikas are of course the Naiyâyikas or followers of the Nyâya. The *Bhâṭṭas* are presumably the disciples of Kumârila Bhaṭṭa, the well-known Mimânsaka already referred to, who lived about a century before Śankara Âchârya.

VII.

The 'withdrawal' (*apavâda*) is the assertion that the whole of the unreal, beginning with Ignorance, which is an illusory effect of the Real, is nothing but the Real; just as a snake, which is the illusory effect of a rope, is nothing whatsoever but the rope.

It has been said, "An actual change of form is called *vikâra*, whilst a merely apparent change of form is called *vivartta*." This shall now be illustrated.

The whole of the four classes of gross bodies constituting the seat of enjoyment,—the food and drink necessary for their use,—the fourteen worlds, Bhûr and the rest, the repository of these,—and Brahma's egg which is the receptacle of all those worlds,—all these are nothing more than the quintuplicated elements of which they are made.

The quintuplicated elements, with sound and the other objects of sense, and the subtile bodies,—all these are nothing more than the non-quintuplicated elements of which they are made.

The non-quintuplicated elements, with the qualities of goodness and the rest, in the inverse order of their production, are nothing more than Ignorance-associated Intelligence, which is their material cause.

Ignorance,[1] and Intelligence associated with it, constituting Îśwara, &c., are nothing more than Brahma, the Fourth, the unassociated Intelligence, which forms their substrate.

[1] How can *Ignorance* be "nothing more than Brahma," seeing that it is an eternally distinct "entity"?

NOTE ON SECTION VII.

The object of the foregoing is to demonstrate that the phenomenal world is nought but the illusory effect (*vivartta*) of the secondless Reality Brahma, who is its illusory material cause. The relation between Brahma and the phenomenal is that of the rope mistaken for a snake, which snake is only an illusion. *Vikâra*, on the other hand, which is synonymous with *pariṇâma* (*Amara*, iii. 2. 15), is a real change of form and name. Instances of it are found in the formation of an earring from a lump of gold, or of a jar or toy-elephant from clay, in which there is a change of form and of name, but not of substance; or in the transformation of milk into curds, where there is a change of substance as well as of name and form.

The old Vedantists, as already stated, regarded the phenomenal world as a *vikâra* or evolution from Brahma, a view which is strenuously rejected by the moderns[1] or *mâyâvâdins*.

[1] Their doctrine of existences, already stated, must be borne in mind here.

VIII.

By means of these two, illusory attribution and its withdrawal, the precise meaning of the words 'That' and 'Thou' [in the sentence 'That art Thou,' '*tat twam asi*'] is determined.

For example, the collective aggregate of Ignorance and the rest, Intelligence associated with it and having the characteristic of omniscience, &c. [*i.e.*, Îśwara], and the unassociated Intelligence,—this triad, appearing as one, after the manner of a red-hot iron ball [where the iron and the fire are not viewed as distinct], is the literal [or expressed] meaning of the word 'That;' but, unassociated Intelligence, the substrate of that which is associated, is its real [or indicated] meaning.

The distributive aggregate of Ignorance and the rest, Intelligence associated with it and having the characteristic of limited knowledge [*i.e.*, Prâjna], and Intelligence which is not associated,—this triad, appearing as one, after the manner of a red-hot ball of iron, is the literal meaning of the word 'Thou;' but, pure Intelligence, the Fourth, all-pervading joy, the substrate of that associated Intelligence, is its real meaning.

NOTE ON SECTION VIII.

This section prepares the way for the subject to the consideration of which the two succeeding sections are devoted, namely, the identity in meaning of the terms 'That' and 'Thou' in the great Vedantic sentence 'That art Thou.'

"If they cannot be shown to mean the same thing, then the sentence does not enunciate a truth. The author therefore undertakes to show that they do mean the same thing. This he does by showing, as we have just seen, that the only apparent difference between the senses of the two terms is that which appears to exist between Ignorance in its *collective* aggregate and Ignorance in its *distributive* aggregate; and as it has been ruled that these have *no* difference—as there is none between a forest and its trees—it follows that there is no difference in meaning between the term 'That' and the term 'Thou' in the sentence 'That art Thou.'"[1]

[1] *Lecture on the Vedânta.*

IX.

Now the great sentence shall be explained.

This sentence, 'That art Thou,' viewed under three different relations, declares what is meant by the Indivisible [or Impartite].

The three relations are—

(a.) The community of reference (*sâmânâdhikaraṇya*) of the two words ['That' and 'Thou'].

(b.) The position of predicate and subject (*viśeshaṇa-viśeshyabhâva*) occupied by the things referred to by the words,—and

(c.) The connection as indicated and indicator (*lakshya-lakshaṇabhâva*), between the purport of the two words and individuated self.

As it has been said, "Between the things which the words refer to, and individuated self (*pratyagâtman*), there is community of reference, the connection as predicate and subject, and as indicated and indicator."[1]

(a.) *Community of reference.*

As, in the sentence 'That is this same Devadatta,'[2] the words 'that' and 'this,' which respectively distinguish the Devadatta of a former and of the present time, are connected by the fact that they both refer to one and the same Devadatta;—so, in the sentence 'That art Thou,' the words 'That' and 'Thou,' which indicate Intelligence characterised respectively by invisibility and visibility, have the connection of reference to one and the same Intelligence.

(b.) *Connection as predicate and subject.*

As, in that same sentence ['That is this same D.'], the relation of predicate and subject exists between the Devadatta of the former time, who is referred to in the word 'That,' and the Devadatta of the present time, referred to in the word 'this,'—a relation constituted by the exclusion of the difference [of time] which there is between them,—so, too, in this sentence ['That art Thou'] is there the relation of predicate and subject be-

[1] *Naishkarmyasiddhi*, iii. 3.

[2] *I.e.*, 'That person whom I saw on some former occasion is this same Devadatta whom I now behold.'—Ballantyne's *Lecture on the Vedânta.*

tween Intelligence distinguished by invisibility, as indicated by the word 'That,' and Intelligence distinguished by visibility, as indicated by the word 'Thou,'—a relation constituted by the exclusion of the difference which there is between them.

(c.) *Connection as indicator and indicated.*

As in that sentence ['That is this D.'], by the omission of the contradictory characteristics of former and present time, the words 'that' and 'this,' or the things they refer to, hold the relation of indicator and indicated with respect to the non-contradictory [or common] term 'Devadatta;'—so, too, in this sentence ['That art Thou'], by the omission of the conflicting characteristics of invisibility and visibility, the words 'That' and 'Thou,' or the things represented by them, hold the relation of indicator and indicated with respect to the non-conflicting [or common] term 'Intelligence.'

This is what is called [in Alankâra] 'the indication of a portion'[1] (*bhâgalakshaṇâ*).

[1] Cf. *Adhyâtma Râmâyaṇa-Uttarakâṇḍa*, v. 27.

NOTE ON SECTION IX.

Bhâgalakshaṇâ.

According to Hindu rhetoricians, the meaning of every word or sentence comes under one of three heads, that is, it is either literal (*vâchya*), indicative (*lakshya*), or suggestive (*vyangya*). Their three functions or powers are termed Denotation (*abhidhâ*), Indication (*lakshaṇâ*), and Suggestion (*vyanjanâ*). We are here concerned with the middle one only, which is thus defined in the *Kâvyaprakâśa* (ii. 9): "When the literal meaning is incompatible [with the rest of the sentence], and, either from usage or from some motive, another meaning is indicated, in connection with the primary one, that imposed function is called 'Indication.'"

The sentence "A herd-station on the Ganges" is an example of this. Here the *literal* meaning of the word 'Ganges' is *incompatible* with the rest of the sentence, it being impossible that the herdsmen could be living on the surface of the water; so it is clear that the river's 'bank' is *indicated*, and this meaning is *imposed* upon the word 'Ganges' in accordance with *usage*. In using the word 'Ganges' rather than 'bank of the Ganges,' there is also the *motive* of conveying the idea of coolness, purity, &c., which might not be equally well suggested by the use of the latter expression.

There are numerous varieties of 'Indication'—according to the author of the *Sâhityadarpaṇa*, there are as many as eighty—but the two principal ones, and those which alone concern us, are—

(1.) Inclusive Indication (*upâdâna-lakshaṇâ*), and

(2.) Indicative Indication (*lakshaṇa-lakshaṇâ*).

The former is described in the *Kâvyaprakâśa* (ii. 10) as that which introduces something else in order to establish itself, and the latter as that which abandons itself in order to introduce something else.

An example of 'Inclusive Indication' is "The white is galloping," the literal sense of which is impossible, whilst what is indicated is "The white *horse* is galloping." Thus the word 'horse' is introduced without the abandonment of the term 'white.' This class is therefore sometimes called '*ajahatswârthâ*' or '*ajahallakshaṇâ*,' Indication in which there is the use of a word *without* the abandonment of its sense.

An example of 'Indicative Indication,' or Indication simply, is the sentence already given, "A herd-station on the Ganges," where the word 'Ganges' abandons its own meaning in order to introduce that of the 'bank.' This class is therefore sometimes called '*jahatswârthâ*,' or '*jahallakshaṇâ*,' Indication in which there is the use of a word *with* the abandonment of its meaning.

Now the *bhâgalakshaṇâ* of the text is a combination of these two varieties, and is therefore otherwise called *jahadajahallakshaṇâ*. This term is defined in the *Vâchaspatya* as "Indication abiding in one part of the expressed meaning, whilst another part of it is abandoned. As, for example, in the sentence 'That is this Devadatta,' whilst the meanings expressive of past and present time are abandoned, another portion of the expressed meaning remains and conveys the idea of the one Devadatta. And again, in the sentence 'That art thou, Śwetaketu,' whilst there is the abandonment of the conflicting ideas of omniscience and parviscience, there is, as in the other example, the retention of one portion which conveys the idea of Intelligence only."[1]

These two varieties of Indication must be thoroughly understood in order to comprehend the purport of the following Section.

[1] *Vide Vâchaspatya*, s.v. *Jahadajahallakshaṇâ.*

X.

In the sentence 'That art Thou,' the *literal* meaning is not suitable as it is in such a sentence as 'The lotus is blue.' For, in the latter, the literal sense suits because there is no valid reason for not accepting the fact that the quality denoted by the term 'blue,' and the substance denoted by the term 'lotus,'—inasmuch as they exclude such other qualities and substances as 'white' and 'cloth,'—are mutually connected as subject and predicate, or are identical, each being qualified by the other.[1]

But, in the former sentence, the literal meaning does not suit, because there is the evidence of our senses against the acceptance of a connection as subject and predicate, between Intelligence distinguished by invisibility as denoted by the term 'That,' and Intelligence distinguished by visibility as denoted by the term 'Thou,'—a connection constituted by the exclusion of their mutual differences

[1] The 'lotus' being the thing that we call 'blue,' and the 'blue' thing being what we call 'lotus.'—*Ballantyne.*

(page 85);—and also against our regarding them as identical, each being qualified by the other.

Nor, again, is it consistent to regard it as an example of 'Indication in which the primary sense is abandoned'[1] (*jahallakshaṇá*), as is the case in the sentence 'The herdsman lives on the Ganges.' For, as the literal sense, which places the Ganges and the herdsman in the relation of location and thing located, is altogether incongruous, whilst an appropriate sense is obtained by abandoning the literal meaning altogether and regarding it as indicating the 'bank' connected with it,—it is rightly regarded as an example of 'Indication in which the primary sense is abandoned.'

But, in the other case, as the literal sense, which expresses the identity of the Intelligences characterised severally by invisibility and visibility, is only partially incongruous,—and as, unless we abandon the remaining part, it would be inappropriate to consider something else to be indicated, —it is not proper to regard it as an instance of 'Indication in which the primary sense is abandoned.'

And it must not be said, "As the word

[1] *Vide* Note on preceding Section.

'Ganges' abandons its own meaning and indicates the 'bank,' so let the word 'That' or 'Thou' abandon its own meaning and indicate the word 'Thou' or 'That,' and then *jahallakshaṇâ* would not be incongruous." For, in the one case, as there is no distinct notion of the word 'bank,' because it is not heard, there is need for the conveyance of that notion by Indication; but as the words 'That' and 'Thou' *are* heard, and there is a distinct perception of their sense, there is no need of the reconveyance of the perception of the sense of each by the other, by means of Indication.

Further, it cannot be regarded as an instance of '*ajahallakshaṇâ*,' as is the case in the sentence "The red is running."[1] For, as the literal sense, which denotes the motion of the quality 'red,' is incongruous, whilst it is possible to avoid that incongruity by perceiving that a 'horse,' or other animal, is indicated as the seat of the redness, without the abandonment of the term 'red,'—it is right to regard it as an instance of 'Indication in which the primary sense is not abandoned' (*ajahallakshaṇâ*).

[1] *Vide* Note on preceding Section.

But, in the other case, as the literal sense, namely, the identity of the Intelligences distinguished severally by invisibility and visibility, is incongruous, and the incongruity is not removed by regarding something else connected therewith as indicated without the abandonment of the contradictory terms, the sentence does not stand as an example of that kind of Indication.

And it must not be said, "Let the word 'That' or 'Thou' abandon the incongruous portion of its meaning,[1] and, retaining the other portion,[2] indicate the meaning of the word 'Thou' or 'That'[3] respectively; then there will be no need of explaining it in another way as '*bhâgalakshaṇâ*' or the 'Indication of a portion.'" For it is impossible for one word to indicate a portion of its own meaning and the meaning of another word; and, further, there is no expectation of the perception of the meaning of either word again by means of Indication, when its meaning has been already perceived by the use of a separate word.

Therefore, as, on account of the incongruity of

[1] Viz., that of invisibility or visibility, respectively.

[2] Viz., that of Intelligence.

[3] *I.e.*, Intelligence characterised by parviscience, &c., or by omniscience, &c., respectively.

a portion of its literal meaning which denotes a Devadatta who is distinguished by both past and present time, the sentence 'That is this Devadatta,' or its purport, by abandoning the portion characterised by the contradictory terms past and present time, indicates merely the non-contradictory portion, namely, Devadatta himself,—so, in like manner, on account of the incongruity of a portion of its literal sense which denotes the identity of Intelligences characterised by invisibility and visibility, the sentence 'That art Thou,' or its purport, abandons the portion characterised by the conflicting terms invisibility and visibility, and indicates merely the non-conflicting portion, namely, the Indivisible Intelligence.

NOTE ON SECTION X.

"This view of the matter may be illustrated algebraically. Not being able to admit as an equation the expression 'Devadatta + past time = Devadatta + present time,' we reflect that the conception of *time* is not essential to the conception of D's nature; and we strike it out of both sides of the expression, which then gives 'Devadatta = Devadatta,' the equality being that of identity. In the same way, not being able to admit as an equation the expression 'Soul + invisibility = Soul + visibility,' we reflect that the visibility, &c., are but the modifications of Ignorance, which, we were told, is no 'reality.' Deleting the unessential portion of each side of the expression, we find 'Soul = Soul,' the equality being here also that of identity."[1]

It must be understood that this Section is closely connected with the Ninth, and must be read with it. The two are here disconnected in order to introduce the explanation of a technicality.

[1] *Lecture on the Vedânta.*

XI.

THE meaning of the sentence "I am Brahma," [the expression of] the experience [of the instructed pupil] shall now be explained.

When, after making clear the meaning of the words 'That' and 'Thou' by means of the erroneous attribution and its subsequent withdrawal, the teacher has communicated the meaning of the Indivisible by means of the sentence ['That art Thou'], then a modification of the internal organ (*chittavṛitti*) assuming the form of the Indivisible, arises within the qualified person, and he says, "I am Brahma, the unchanging, pure, intelligent, free, undecaying, supreme joy, eternal, secondless."

That modification of the internal organ, being accompanied by the reflection of Intelligence, and being directed towards the previously unrecognised Supreme Brahma, non-different from individuated self, drives away the ignorance which invests him.

Then, as, when the threads composing a piece of cloth are burned, the cloth itself is consumed, so, when Ignorance, the cause of all effects, is destroyed, every effect ceases; and therefore the modification of the internal organ which has assumed the form of the Indivisible, being one of those effects, also ceases.

As the light of a lamp, unable to illuminate the sun's light, is overpowered by it, so, too, the Intelligence which is there reflected in that modification of the internal organ being incapable of illuminating the Supreme Brahma, non-different from individuated self, is overpowered by it; and its associate, the modification of the internal organ [shaped] on the Indivisible, having been destroyed, it becomes [*i.e.*, merges into] the Supreme Brahma, non-different from individuated self; just as, on the removal of a mirror, the face reflected in it lapses into the face itself.

Such being the case, the two Vedic sayings, "He [Brahma] is to be perceived by the mind alone,"[1] and "He [Brahma] whom with the mind one thinks not,"[2] are not contradictory. For whilst the need of the pervasion by the modification of the

[1] *Bṛihadâraṇyaka*, vi. 4. 19. [2] *Kenopanishad*, i. 5.

internal organ is admitted, [for the cognition of the veiled Brahma, as of other unknown objects], the need of its pervading the result [viz., the unveiled Brahma] is denied. As it has been said,[1] "For the removal of the ignorance [resting] on Brahma, its pervasion by the modification of the internal organ is requisite; but the authors of the Śâstras deny that [in His case] there is need of its pervading the result." For, "As Brahma is self-luminous, the light [necessary for illuminating the jar, &c.] is not employed [in His case]."[2]

When the modification of the internal organ assumes the shape of an *inanimate* object, the case is different. For example, [in the cognition] 'This is a jar,' the modification of the internal organ which assumes the shape of the jar is directed towards the unknown object, jar, removes the ignorance which rests on it, and, at the same time, illuminates it, though insentient, with the light of its own indwelling Intelligence. As it has been said,[3] "The internal organ and the light of Intelligence abiding in it, both pervade the jar; then, the ignorance [covering the jar] disappears by means of the former, whilst the jar bursts forth by means

[1] ?

[2] ?

[3] ?

of the latter." Just as the light of a lamp directed towards a jar or other object standing in the dark dispels the darkness enveloping it, and by its own brilliance brings it to view.[1]

[1] In the passage at the top of the preceding page, I have taken the word *vyâpyatwa* in a non-technical sense on the authority of the commentary *Subodhinî*, which reads thus :—" *Antahkaraṇavṛittir âvaraṇanivṛittyartham ajnânâvachchhinnachaitanyam vyâpnotîtyetadvṛittivyâpyatwam angîkriyate* | *Âvaraṇabhangânantaram swayam prakâśamânam chaitanyam phalachaitanyam ityuchyate, asmin phalachaitanye nishkalanke chittavrittir na vyâpnoti, âvaraṇabhangasya prâgeva jâtatwena prayojanâbhâvâd ityarthah* | " "The modification of the internal organ pervades the ignorance-appropriated Intelligence, in order to remove the covering, and the need of that pervasion is admitted. The Intelligence that shines forth of itself after the destruction of the covering is called '*phalachaitanya ;*' the modification of the internal organ does not pervade that spotless *phalachaitanya*, for, since it existed before the destruction of the covering, such pervasion is unnecessary."

NOTE ON SECTION XI.

From this passage we learn that when the meaning of the great sentence 'That art Thou' has been explained to the pupil and understood by him, he perceives the Indivisible and realises his oneness with Him.

According to the Vedânta, perception of an object, such as a jar, takes place in the following way. When the eye is fixed upon the jar, the internal organ, with the Intelligence appropriated to or reflected in it, goes out towards it, and by its light dispels the darkness of Ignorance enveloping it, illuminates it, *assumes its shape*, and so cognises it. The stock illustration of this is that of water flowing from a well or tank by means of a narrow open channel, emptying itself into the square beds with raised edges, into which a field is sometimes divided for the purpose of irrigation, and assuming the shape of those beds. The illuminated internal organ is the water, and the operation is called an evolution or 'modification' of that organ. As pointed out in the text, however, the perception of Brahma differs from that of an ordinary object, in that He, being self-luminous, is not revealed by the light of the Intelligence reflected in the internal organ, but shines forth as soon as the latter has dispelled the Ignorance enveloping Him.

The word which I have here rendered 'internal organ' is more properly 'thought,' which is a component part of that organ. (See page 68.)

XII.

As, up to the time of the immediate cognition of Intelligence, which is his own essence, it is necessary to practise (a.) hearing (*śravaṇa*), (b.) consideration (*manana*), (c.) profound contemplation (*nididhyâsana*), and (d.) meditation (*samâdhi*), these are now set forth.

(a.) 'Hearing' is the ascertaining of the drift of all the Vedantic writings regarding the secondless Reality, by the use of the sixfold means of knowledge[1] (*linga*). These means are (1) the beginning and the ending, (2) repetition, (3) novelty, (4) the result, (5) persuasion, and (6) illustration from analogy. As it has been said,[2] "The beginning and the ending, repetition, novelty, the result, persuasion, and illustration from analogy, are the means for the determination of the purport."

1. 'The beginning and the ending' (*upakra-*

[1] *Lingam artham gamayati.* Sch.

mopasamhârau) are the mention at the beginning and end of a chapter of the subject to be expounded in it; as in the 6th chapter of the Chhândogya Upanishad, at the beginning of which, the secondless Reality who is to be set forth in it, is declared in the words "One only without a second," and, at the end, in the words "All this is the essence of That."

2. 'Repetition' (*abhyâsa*) is the repeated declaration in a chapter of the subject which is to be set forth in it; as, for example, in that same chapter, the secondless Reality is set forth nine times in the words "That art Thou."

3. 'Novelty' (*apûrvatâ*) is the fact that the subject to be treated of in a chapter is not an object of perception by any other means; as, for example, in that same chapter, the secondless Reality [there set forth] is not an object of perception by any other means.

4. 'The result' (*phala*) is the motive, set forth in various places, for acquiring the knowledge of Self who is to be treated of in a chapter, or for carrying that knowledge into practice; as, for example, in that same chapter (vi. 14, 2), where it says, "The man who has a teacher knows [the

truth], but he is delayed [from absorption] until he is set free [by death]; then he attains to it,"—the acquisition of the secondless Reality is set forth as the motive for acquiring the knowledge of Him.

5. 'Persuasion'[1] (*arthavâda*) is the praising, in various places, the subject to be treated of in a chapter; just as, in that same chapter (vi. 1, 3), the secondless Reality is praised in these words,—"Didst thou ask for that instruction by which the unheard of becomes heard;—the unthought, thought,—the unknown, known?"

6. 'Illustration from analogy' (*upapatti*) is an argument stated in various places in support of the subject to be treated of in a chapter; as, for example, in that same chapter (vi. 1, 4), in demonstrating the secondless Reality, an argument is set forth as follows, to show that the variety of forms [in the universe] rests upon a foundation of words[2] and nothing else,—"O, gentle one! as, by means of one lump of earth, everything earthen is known

[1] "'Persuasion' is the setting forth of the end, *i.e.*, of the motive; that is to say, it is a speech intended to commend the object of an injunction. For a persuasive speech, by means of laudation, &c., commends the object of an injunction with a view to our quickly engaging [in the performance of the ceremony enjoined]."—Ballantyne's *Aphorisms of the Nyâya*, ii. 63 (b).

[2] *Vâchârambhaṇa*=*vâgâlambana*. (*Bhâshya* on the *Upanishad*).

to be a thing resting upon words alone, a change of form, a name, and nothing in reality but earth, [so is it with the phenomenal world which is nought but Brahma]."

(b.) 'Consideration' is unceasing reflection on the secondless Reality which has been heard of, in conjunction with arguments in support of the Vedânta.

(c.) 'Profound contemplation' is the continuance of ideas consistent with the secondless Reality, to the exclusion of the notion of body and suchlike things which are inconsistent [with Him].

(d.) 'Meditation' is of two kinds, viz. :—

1. *With* recognition of subject and object (*savikalpaka*), and

2. *Without* such recognition (*nirvikalpaka*).

(1.) 'Meditation with the recognition of subject and object' is the resting of the modification of the internal organ on the secondless Reality whose shape it has assumed, *without* any concern as to the merging of the distinction between the knower and the knowledge, &c. Then, just as there is the perception of earth [and of that alone], even though there be the appearance of an earthen toy-elephant, &c., so too is there the perception of the secondless

Reality [alone], even though there be the appearance of duality. As it has been said by those engaged [in such contemplation]:—"I am that secondless one who is ever free, whose essence is knowledge, like the ether [*i.e.*, pure and formless], supreme, once seen [that is, never changing, as the moon, &c., does], unborn, alone, everlasting, undefiled [by contact with Ignorance, &c.], all-pervading; I am pure knowledge, whose essence is unvariableness; I am neither fettered nor set free" (*Upadeśasahasrî*, verses 73 and 74).

(2.) 'Meditation without the recognition of subject and object' is the resting of the modification of the understanding on the secondless Reality whose shape it has assumed, *with* concern as to the merging of the distinction of knower and knowledge, &c., so as to be completely identified with Him. Then, just as, owing to the disappearance of salt after it has [melted and so] assumed the shape of the water [into which it was thrown], nothing appears but the water,[1] so, by the disappearance of the modification of the internal organ after it has assumed the shape of the secondless Reality, nothing appears but the latter.

[1] Compare *Chhândogya Upanishad*, vi. 13.

It must not be supposed that this state and sound sleep are identical; for, though in both alike the modification of the internal organ is not perceived, there is nevertheless this one distinction between them, that it is present in the former [though unperceived], but not in the latter.[1]

[1] *Rational Refutation*, p. 224, but cf. *Yoga Aphorisms*, i. 10.

NOTES ON SECTION XII.

1. '*Profound contemplation is,*' &c.

I am doubtful of this rendering. The text of the Calcutta edition of 1875 stands thus:—*Vijâtîyadehâdipratyayarahitâdwitîyavastusajâtîyapratyayapravâhah nididhyâsanam.* That used by Dr. Ballantyne, and adopted too in the St. Petersburg edition of 1877, reads as follows:—*Vijâtîyadehâdipratyayarahitâdvitîyavastuni tadâkârâkâritâyâ buddheh sajâtîyapravâho nididhyâsanam.* It is thus translated by Dr. Ballantyne: "'Contemplation' is the homogeneous flow of the understanding mirroring its object, when this object is the Real, &c., to the exclusion of the notion of body or any other thing heterogeneous [to the one Reality mirrored in the understanding]."

2. '*I am the secondless one,*' &c.

This passage is a quotation from Śankarâchârya's *Upadeśasahasrî*, but it is also found in the closing portion of the *Muktikopanishad.* The opening verses of this Upanishad, which is said to belong to the White Yajur Veda (!), introduce us to a scene 'in the charming city of Ayodhyâ,' where Râma, attended by Sîtâ, his brothers, and various sages, is addressed by Mâruti, as the Supreme Self, the embodiment of existence, intelligence, and joy, and is asked to make known to him the way of escape from the fetters of transmigration. The sectarianism and style of this Upanishad stamp it as modern;[1] and it doubtless copied from the *Upadeśasahasrî*, not only the passage

[1] See Weber's *History of Indian Literature*, p. 165.

quoted in our text, but other verses in immediate connection with it.

The author of the Vedântasâra does not cite the passage as a quotation from the Veda, as he invariably does when quoting from an Upanishad, but ushers it in with the words '*taduktam abhiyuktaih.*'

The passage as given in the Vedântasâra differs in some respects from the original, as will be seen by comparing the two.

Upadeśasahasrî.

Dṛiśisvarûpam gaganopamam param
Sakṛidvibhâtam tvajamekam aksharam |
Alepakam sarvagatam yadadwyam
Tadeva châham satatam vimukta Om || 73

Dṛiśistu śuddho 'hamavikriyâtmako
Na me 'sti kaśchidvishayah svabhâvatah |
[*Purastiraśchordhvamadhaścha sarvatah*
Sampûrṇabhûmâ tvaja âtmani sthitah] || 74.

Vedântasâra (Calc. 1875).

Dṛiśisvarûpam gaganopamam param
Sakṛidvibhâtam tvajam ekam avyayam |
Alepakam sarvagatam yadadwyam
Tadeva châham satatam vimuktam ||
Dṛiśistu suddho 'ham avikriyâtmako
Na me 'sti bandho na cha me vimokshah | .

The actual reading in the last line is *baddho,* which is clearly a misprint.

3. For various explanations of the technical terms

savikalpaka and *nirvikalpaka*,[1] see Ballantyne's *Tarka-sangraha* (2d edition), para. 46; Translation of *Sâhitya Darpaṇa*, p. 52 (note); and Cowell's Translation of *Kusumânjali*, p. 20 (note).

[1] With these two kinds of meditation compare the '*samprajnâta*' and '*asamprajnâta*' of the Yoga philosophy. The former is 'meditation with an object,' and the latter 'meditation without an object.'

XIII.

THE means [to *nirvikalpaka* meditation] are—

1. Forbearance (*yama*).
2. Minor religious observances (*niyama*).
3. Religious postures (*âsana*).
4. Regulation of the breath (*prâṇâyâma*).
5. Restraint of the organs of sense (*pratyâhâra*).
6. Fixed attention (*dhâraṇâ*).
7. Contemplation (*dhyâna*).
8. Meditation (*samâdhi*).

1. Acts of 'forbearance' are, sparing life, truthfulness, not stealing, chastity, and non-acceptance of gifts (*aparigraha*).[1]

2. 'Minor religious observances' are, purification, contentment, endurance of hardships, inaudible repetition of sacred texts (*svâdhyâya*), and concentration of the thoughts on Îśwara.

[1] *Bhogasâdhanânâm anangîkârah.* Bhojarâja on *Yoga*, ii. 30.

3. The 'religious postures' are distinguished by particular positions of the hands and feet, such as *Padmâsana, Svastikâsana,* and others.

4. 'Regulation of the breath' consists of the methods of restraining it known as *rechaka, pûraka,* and *kumbhaka.*

5. 'Restraint of the organs of sense' is the holding them back from their several objects of sense.

6. 'Fixed attention' is the fixing of the internal organ upon the secondless Reality.

7. 'Contemplation' is the continuing of the modification of the internal organ upon the secondless Reality, at intervals.

8. 'Meditation' is that already described as accompanied by the recognition of subject and object (*savikalpaka*).

To the meditation without recognition of subject and object, to which the above are subservient, there are four obstacles, viz.—

1. Mental inactivity (*laya*).
2. Distraction (*vikshepa*).
3. Passion (*kashâya*), and
4. The tasting of enjoyment (*rasâswâda*).

1. 'Mental inactivity' is the drowsiness of the modification of the internal organ while not resting on the secondless Reality.

2. 'Distraction' is the resting of the modification of the internal organ on something else, instead of its abiding on the secondless Reality.

3. 'Passion' is the not resting on the secondless Reality, by reason of the impeding of the modification of the internal organ by lust or other desire, even though there be no mental inactivity or distraction.

4. The 'tasting of enjoyment' is the experience of pleasure on the part of the modification of the internal organ, in the recognition of subject and object, while it is not resting on the secondless Reality; or it is the experiencing of such pleasure when about to commence meditation without the recognition of subject and object.

When the internal organ, free from these four hindrances, and motionless as a lamp sheltered from the wind, exists as the indivisible Intelligence only, then is realised that which is called meditation without recognition of subject and object.

It has been said,[1] "When the internal organ

[1] *Gauḍapâda's Kârikâs*, iii. 44, 45.

has fallen into a state of inactivity, one should arouse it,—when it is distracted, one should render it quiescent [by turning away from objects of sense, &c.],—when it is affected by passion, one should realise the fact,—when quiescent, one should not disturb it. One should experience no pleasure [during discriminative meditation], but become free from attachment by means of discriminative intelligence." And again[1]—"As [the flame of] a lamp standing in a sheltered spot flickers not," &c.

[1] *Bhagavadgîtâ*, vi. 19. The whole verse is—"As [the flame of] a lamp standing in a sheltered spot flickers not, this is regarded as an illustration of a mind-restrained Yogî who is practising concentration of mind."

NOTES ON SECTION XIII.

The eight means of promoting *nirvikalpaka* meditation, which are enumerated in the text, are taken from the Yoga Aphorisms, ii. 29; and the definitions of the eight are from the same source, namely, ii. 30–53, and iii. 1–3. The first two, *yama* and *niyama*, are also described in Manu iv. 204 (Sch.).

'*Religious postures.*'

Padmâsana is thus described by Professor Monier Williams in his Sanskrit Lexicon:—"A particular posture in religious meditation, sitting with the thighs crossed, with one hand resting on the left thigh, the other held up with the thumb upon the heart, and the eyes directed to the tip of the nose." The *Rudrayâmala*, however, defines it as simply sitting with the left foot on the right thigh and the right foot on the left thigh. To this, the *Tantrasâra* adds the following direction:—"*Angushthau cha nibadhnîyâddhastâbhyâm vyutkramât tatah*"—which may possibly mean, "And he should retain the big toes [in their position] by means of the hands in the reverse order," *i.e.*, the left hand on the right foot and the right hand on the left foot (?).

Svastikâsana is described by *Vâchaspatimiśra* as sitting with the left foot doubled up under the right knee and the right foot under the left knee, and the *Tantrasâra* adds that the body must be erect. (Vide *Vâchaspatya* s. v. *âsana.*)

'*Regulation of the breath*' (*prâṇâyâma*).

"The first act is expiration, which is performed through

the right nostril, whilst the left is closed with the fingers of the right hand: this is called *Rechaka*. The thumb is then placed upon the right nostril and the fingers raised from the left, through which breath is inhaled: this is called *Pûraka*. In the third act, both nostrils are closed and breathing suspended: this is *Kumbhaka*. And a succession of these operations is the practice of *Prâṇâyâma*."—(Wilson's *Vishnu Purâṇa*, v. 231.)

XIV.

THE characteristics of the 'liberated but still living' (*jîvanmukta*) are now to be described.

The 'liberated but still living' is he who by knowing the indivisible, pure Brahma, who is his own essence, [a result brought about] by the removal of the Ignorance enveloping Him, perceives Him clearly as the Indivisible and his own essence; and, in consequence of the removal of Ignorance and its effects, such as accumulated works, doubt, and error, remains intent on Brahma,[1] freed from all fetters. As it is said in the Śruti,[2] "When he who is supreme and not supreme (*parâvara*) is seen, the fetter of the heart is burst, all doubts are removed, and works[3] fade away."

On arising from meditation, though he sees

[1] Dr. Hall renders '*brahmanishthah*' by 'abides in Brahma,' but the commentator explains it by '*Brahmaṇi nishṭhâ tadekaparatâ yasya.*'

[2] *Muṇḍakopanishad*, 2. 2. 8.

[3] Those of the present or of a former birth which had not begun to bear fruit; but *not* those which brought about his present existence.—*Bhâshya.*

that, by his body, which is the receptacle of flesh, blood, urine, filth, &c.,—by his organs, which are the seat of blindness, slowness, unskilfulness, &c.,—and by his internal organ, which is the seat of hunger, thirst, sorrow, infatuation, &c.,—works are being done according to the previous bent of each; and that he is experiencing the fruit of those which have already commenced to take effect, and yet his knowledge is not interfered with,—he regards them not as real because they have been cancelled. Just as one watching what he knows to be a conjuring performance does not regard it as a reality. It is said, too, in the Śruti,[1] "Though he has eyes, he is as though he had them not; though he has ears, he is as though he had none; though he has a mind, he is as one without a mind; though he has vital airs, he is as though he had them not." And again it has been said,[2] "He who, when awake, is as though in a sound sleep, and sees not duality, or, if seeing it, regards it as non-duality,—who, though acting, is free from [the results of] actions, he, and he alone, is, without doubt, the knower of Self." Just as he continues the practices of eating, walk-

[1] ?

[2] *Upadeśasahasrī*, verse 85.

ing about, &c., which existed before the attainment of true knowledge, so too he either follows good desires alone, or is indifferent to both good and bad alike. It has been said,[1] "If he who knows the secondless Reality may act as he likes, what difference is there between the knowers of truth and dogs in respect of eating impure food? Except the fact of knowing Brahma, there is no difference; the one knows the Self, and the other [the dog] does not."

In that state, humility, &c., which are means of acquiring right apprehension, and good qualities, such as friendliness, &c., cling to him merely as ornaments. It has been said,[2] "Qualities such as friendliness, and the like, exist without an effort in one who has attained to the knowledge of Self, but are not of the nature of means [to that end]." To conclude:—Experiencing, for the sustentation of his body only, the fruits of works which have begun to take effect, which are characterised by pleasure or pain, and are brought about by his own desire, or without any desire on his part, or at the desire of another,—and illuminating the reflections on his internal organ,—when the fruits of his works

[1] *Naishkarmyasiddhi*, iv. 60. [2] *Ibid.*, iv. 67.

are exhausted, and his vital airs merge in the supreme Brahma who is all-pervading happiness, then, owing to the destruction of Ignorance and also of the germs of its effects, he abides the Indivisible Brahma who is absolute isolation, whose sole essence is joy, and who is free from all appearance of change. As the Śruti says,[1] "His vital airs ascend not" [*i.e.*, do not transmigrate], but are dissolved within him; and[2]—"He already free [though in the body], is freed [from future embodiments]."

[1] *Bṛihadâraṇyaka*, 5. 4. 6 (p. 856).
[2] *Kaṭhopanishad*, v. 1 (p. 133).

NOTES ON SECTION XIV.

1. '*Jîvanmukta.*'

The position of the 'liberated but still living' man closely resembles that of the Buddhist *Arhat* or *Rahat*. At death, the latter enters *Nirwâṇa*, that is, ceases to exist,[1]—whilst the former, absorbed into Brahma, enters upon an unconscious and stone-like existence!

2. '*Works.*'

According to the Systems, works are of three kinds, viz., accumulated (*sanchita*), fructescent (*prârabdha*), and current (*kriyamâṇa*). The first are the works of former births which have not yet borne fruit; the second are those which have resulted in the present life, and so have begun to bear fruit; and the third are those which are being performed during the present life, and which will bear fruit in a future one. According to the Vedânta, the true knowledge of Brahma and of one's own identity with Him burns up the accumulated works and cancels the effects of the current ones. The fruits of the fructescent ones must be exhausted during the present life, and then at death emancipation is realised. These last cannot be destroyed by the knowledge of Brahma; but, according to the Yoga, the meditation which is styled in that system *asamprajnâta*, 'meditation without an object,'[2] *can* destroy them, and so is considered by Yogins to be superior to knowledge.[3]

It will interest the Marâthî student to notice that the com-

[1] Spence Hardy's *Manual of Buddhism*, p. 40, and *Eastern Monachism*, p. 290.

[2] *Aphorisms*, i. 18.

[3] *Rational Refutation*, pp. 30, 31 (*note*).

mon word *prârabdha*, 'fate,' 'destiny,' is just this technical term explained above—works which have begun to take effect, and the fruit of which it is impossible to evade.

3. '*Supreme and not supreme.*'

'Supreme' as cause, 'not supreme' as effect, says the scholiast. It might also be rendered, 'The First and the Last,' that is, the all-inclusive entity. The fetter of the heart consists of desires resulting from Ignorance.

4. '*If he who knows the secondless Reality,*' &c.

This passage, in the original, consists of a verse and a half, and reads as follows:—

Buddhâdvaitasatattvasya yatheshṭâcharaṇam yadi |
Śunâm tattvadṛiśânchaiva ko bhedo 'śuchibhakshaṇe ||
Brahmavittvantathâ muktvâ sa âtmajno na chetarah |

Now the first couplet is also quoted in the *Panchadaśî*, iv. 55, and is ascribed by the scholiast to *Sureśvara*, the reputed disciple of Śankarâchârya; and laboriously following that clue, I at length found the passage in his *Naishkarmyasiddhi*. It is introduced into the *Panchadaśî* in support of an appeal to the enlightened man to avoid evil lest he lose the benefits of his knowledge; and its aim is to show that if one who knows the truth throws off all restraints and acts as he likes, he is no better than a dog. That Sureśvara, too, disapproved of *yatheshṭâcharaṇa* is evident from the context of the passage in question, which I here subjoin:—

"*Athâlepakapakshanirâsârtham âha* | *Buddhâdvaitasatattvasya yatheshṭâcharaṇam yadi* | *śunâm tattvadṛiśâm chaiva ko bhedo 'śuchibhakshaṇe* || 60 || *Kasmânna bhavati yasmât* | *Adharmâj-jâyate 'jnânam yatheshtâcharaṇam tatah* | *dharmakârye katham tat syâdyatra dharmopi neshyate* || 61 || . . . *Tishṭhatu tâvat sarvapravrittibîjaghasmaram jnânam, mumukshvavasthâyâm api na sambhavati yateshṭâcharaṇam* | *Tadâha* | *Yo hi yatra viraktah syânnâsau tasmai pravarttate* | *lokatrayaviraktatwân mumukshuh kimitîhate* || 63 ||

The other half couplet, however, of our text, which, be it observed, is *not* Sureśvara's, seems to reverse this teaching, and to inculcate the doctrine that the knower of Brahma *may* act as he likes with impunity. I fear that this is really the drift of much of the pantheistic teaching of India, and my opinion is supported by a learned Indian writer, already quoted, who says that "Vedantic authors have boldly asserted that they are subject to no law, no rule, and that there is no such thing as virtue or vice, injunction or prohibition." [1]

That there are many passages in the Upanishads and elsewhere which teach this, the accompanying extract from an article by Professor Gough will show :—" The Theosophist liberated from metempsychosis, but still in the body, is untouched by merit and demerit, absolved from all works good and evil, unsoiled by sinful works,[2] uninjured by what he has done and by what he has left undone.[3] Good works, like evil works, and like the God that recompenses them, belong to the unreal, to the fictitious duality, the world of semblances. 'Gnosis, once arisen,' says Śankarâchârya in his prolegomena to the Śvetâsvatara, 'requires nothing farther for the realisation of its result, it needs *subsidia* only that it may arise.' Ânandagiri :—'The theosophist, so long as he lives, may do good and evil as he chooses and incur no stain, such is the efficiency of gnosis.' And so in the *Taittirîya Upanishad* (ii. 9) we read—'The

[1] *Dialogues on Hindu Philosophy*, p. 381.

[2] *Brihadâraṇyakopanishad*, 4. 4. 23.

[3] *Ibid.*, 4. 4. 22.

thought afflicts not him, What good have I left undone, what evil done?' And in the *Bṛihadâraṇyaka*[1]—'Here the thief is no more a thief, the Chandâla no more a Chandâla, the Paulkasa no more a Paulkasa, the sacred mendicant no more a sacred mendicant: they are not followed by good works, they are not followed by evil works. For at last the sage has passed beyond all the sorrows of his heart.' Immoral inferences from this doctrine—the quietists of all ages have been taxed with immorality—are thus redargued by Nrisimhasarasvati:—'Some one may say, It will follow from this the theosophist may act as he chooses. That he can act as he pleases cannot be denied in the presence of texts of revelation, traditionary texts, and arguments such as the following: 'Not by matricide, not by parricide.' 'He that does not identify not-self with self, whose inner faculty is unsullied,—he, though he slay these people, neither slays them, nor is slain.' . . . 'He that knows the truth is sullied neither by good actions nor by evil actions.' . . . In answer to all this we reply: True, but as these texts are only eulogistic of the theosophist; it is not intended that he should thus act."[2]

The line of argument adopted by this commentator, and also by other apologists, is unsafe, and does not get rid of the fact that some of the Upanishads, the chief source of the Vedânta doctrine, do, without any qualification, declare that sin and virtue are alike to one who knows Brahma; and the system is therefore rightly charged with immorality. But, independently of such teaching as this, what moral results could possibly be

[1] *Bṛihadâraṇyakopanishad*, 4. 3. 22.
[2] *Calcutta Review* (1878), p. 34.

expected from a system so devoid of motives for a life of true purity? The Supreme Being, Brahma, is a cold Impersonality, out of relation with the world, unconscious of His own existence and of ours, and devoid of all attributes and qualities. The so-called personal God, the first manifestation of the Impersonal, turns out on examination to be a myth; there is no God apart from ourselves, no Creator, no Holy Being, no Father, no Judge—no one, in a word, to adore, to love, or to fear. And as for ourselves, we are only unreal actors on the semblance of a stage!

The goal, already referred to, is worthy of such a creed, being no less than the complete extinction of all spiritual, mental, and bodily powers by absorption into the Impersonal.

"Annihilation, then, as regards individuals, is as much the ultimate destiny of the soul as it is of the body, and '*Not to be*' is the melancholy result of the religion and philosophy of the Hindus."[1]

5. '*He already free, is freed.*'

"Though illusion has not really real existence, yet it possesses apparent existence, and so it is capable of taking the soul captive. And again, the Vedântins say, that as illusion is only apparent, so the soul's being fettered is practical; that is, as illusion is false, so the soul's being fettered is likewise false. Neither was the soul ever actually fettered, nor is it now fettered, nor has it to be emancipated."[2]

This matter is also explained in the last chapter of the *Vedânta-paribhâshâ*:—" The joy which admits of no in-

[1] Wilson's *Essays on the Religion of the Hindus*, ii. 114.

[2] *Rational Refutation*, p. 189.

crease, is Brahma; as the Veda says, 'He knew Brahma to be joy.' The acquisition of Brahma, whose essence is joy, is *moksha*, and it is also the cessation of sorrow; as the Veda says, 'The knower of Brahma becomes Brahma,' and again, 'The knower of Self passes beyond sorrow.' The acquisition of another world, or the sensuous joy derivable therefrom, is not *moksha;* for as it is the result of works, and therefore non-eternal, the subject of such liberation is liable to future births. If you say that, as, even according to our view, the acquisition of bliss and the cessation of misery have a beginning, they are therefore chargeable with the same defect [*i.e.*, of being non-eternal and therefore transitory], I reply, Not so; for, although *moksha*, consisting of Brahma, is already in possession, still, because of the erroneous idea that it is not possessed, it is proper to make use of means for attaining it. The cessation of misery, too, in the form of Brahma, who is the substrate of all, is already an accomplished fact. Even in mundane affairs, however, we see the need of obtaining things already obtained, and of removing things already removed. For example, when a piece of gold is in one's hand, but has been forgotten [and is being searched for], and some person says, 'Why, the gold is in your hand,' one regains it as if it had not already been in possession. So, too, in the case of one who is under the delusion that the garland encircling his ankle is a snake; when a reliable person tells him that it is not a snake, the snake is removed although it was already removed [*i.e.*, had never existed]. In like manner, the acquisition of a joy already possessed, and the cessation of misery already removed, in other words, *liberation*, is an object [to be sought after]."

INDEX.

PRINTED BY BALLANTYNE, HANSON AND CO.
EDINBURGH AND LONDON